THE PULSE OF LIFE
Understanding Your Life
Through the Rhythms of Nature

Born in America in 1944, Ra (Ron) Bonewitz trained and worked as a geologist, before discovering his latent abilities as a trance medium and a healer. He now lives in London and works as a personal and business consultant, as well as giving lectures and seminars all over the world.

THE PULSE OF LIFE

Understanding Your Life
Through the Rhythms of Nature

Ra Bonewitz   PhD

E L E M E N T   B O O K S

First published in Great Britain in 1988 by
Element Books Limited
Longmead, Shaftesbury, Dorset

Printed and bound in Great Britain by
Billings, Hylton Road, Worcester

Cover design by Max Fairbrother

Text design by Clarke Williams

Cover illustration by Image Bank/Alec Hitchins

British Library Cataloguing in Publication Data

Bonewitz, Ra, *1945–*
The pulse of life : understanding your
life through the rhythms of nature.
1. Man. Rhythms. Occult aspects.
I. Title
133

ISBN 1–85230–037–X

*To Lilian: wherever your path
may take you in this world or others,
my love will walk with you always.*

*A special thanks to Godfrey Thomas, whose help at a
time of crisis made it possible to
write this book.*

Contents

Prologue

All things in the Universe move in rhythms and cycles – the changing seasons, the movement of planets, the birth and death of stars, your own changing realisation of who you really are.

Your own life moves in a very distinct set of patterns and rhythms, leading potentially to self-realisation. However, each stage requires a breaking of the mould, risking the unknown outside our cocoon of old beliefs.

This is a difficult process for everyone, requiring us at each stage to confront our fears and our insecurities. It is usually made more so because we seldom realise what is happening. We often believe that our lives are going dreadfully wrong, when in fact they are going absolutely right.

This book is written to help you see your own patterns, and the patterns of the world around you, and to see that your own growth is part of the Natural Order of the World in which we live.

Introduction

The old saying goes: *When the Student is ready, the Teacher appears*.

To which I add: *The problem is in telling who is who!*

We live in a world of highly complex interactions and relationships, not only with each other, but with all creatures of the Earth, and indeed, with the Earth itself.

This book was written to share my own personal insight and experiences – to be, for a time, the Teacher.

But had I not been the Student, I would have nothing to write.

Yet in the writing of this book, I have learned much . . .

And so the circle goes on.

So, join me now to become for a while, a Student.

Unless, of course, you happen to be a Teacher . . .

With best wishes and blessings
Ra Bonewitz

Woodstock, England
1988

Chapter 1

THE RHYTHMS OF THE UNIVERSE

> If you would contract, first you must expand. If you would weaken, you must first strengthen. If you would take, you must first give. This is called the dawn of intelligence.
>
> LAO TZU (300 BC)

This book focuses on the Unity of all things which live on, and make up, the Earth.

We are creatures of pattern, of rhythm, of cycle – as are our comrades in all the other Kingdoms. How those patterns and rhythms are part of our own, personal pulse of life, is what this book is about.

I wish to demonstrate to you, the reader, that there is a flow, a series of smooth interconnections between all levels of life, and that flow runs in cyclic patterns. Others have said so for thousands of years – the idea is hardly unique to me. But for me, there was the profound realisation that human life was also cyclic and rhythmic, and that those cycles and rhythms followed closely the cycles and rhythms of the natural world around us.

The Tao has stated this for over two thousand years. Yet for our left brain orientated society, the 'proof' is only just available. As it sees the interconnection of all things, permission is given to the other part of ourselves to *feel* the interconnections. For much of the West, the left brain is the doorway to the right – or perhaps a great boulder to roll away from the door of rebirth . . .

In 1983, while attending a course in London given by the Walter Bellin Partnership, I had a total Unity experience.

As a completion of the course, we were doing a guided process (also known as a guided meditation and visualisation) to music. This involved shedding all anger, hatred, grief and so on from our previously incomplete relation-

1

ships, gathering it up into bags, and taking it out into space to return it to its Source, the Cosmos.

As we were going out into space, I felt myself expanding, and in a great rush, suddenly I *was* the Universe. I was aware of a great out-pouring of energy from my heart, like a pulsing electric current running down my arms and through my hands. I was totally aware of my physical body, and yet the stars and galaxies *were* my body.

Many things about the Universe came into my awareness at that moment, much of which was the basis for my book *The Cosmic Crystal Spiral*.

Although a few years have passed since the experience, forgotten details of that experience still re-emerge periodically. This is not entirely surprising because in that moment, *I knew everything*. As I later discovered, this experience was identical in many respects to certain near-death experiences, except in only a few such experiences do people return from this all-knowing state with the memory of it in any way intact. People often report remembering that they *knew*, but not being able to recall *what* they knew.

A flash of the memory returned to me, literally in the form of a 'blinding flash', on a course I was teaching about the patterns of human psychological development. In that moment I remembered the intense pulsing sensation, like a great heartbeat of energy from the 'heart' of the Universe. And I realised in that moment that *all* life beats to that pulse.

Life pulses

Pulse, or rhythm, is the fundamental characteristic of all life – the life of the stars and planets, of plants and animals, of you and me, and of the Universe itself.

These pulses repeat and repeat, each repetition being a new cycle of life.

I had already seen this in its broadest form – the parallel spirals of development that were common to Man and the Universe, that was the basis for *The Cosmic Crystal Spiral*.

These spirals are as follows:

THE RHYTHMS OF THE UNIVERSE

The Universe experiences itself as: You experience yourself as:

man –

plants, –
animals

planets –

galaxies –

stars –

particles, atoms, –
minerals

energy (cosmic egg)

man –

young adult –

teenager –

child –

infant –

cells –
embryo

egg

There were two basic realisations behind these spirals:

1. Man is part of a larger set of patterns which ultimately ends with the Universe itself.

2. The patterns of our own development parallel to a high degree the developmental patterns of all Creation, including the Universe itself.

I am not suggesting that there is an exact correspondence between each turn of the spiral as drawn, but the idea is clear: we and the Universe follow similar patterns of growth and evolution.

Pulse connects all levels of life to itself

Your life, my life, all lives, are part of a great pulsing body of energy that *is* the Universe. Our own lives are part of the intricate interweaving pattern that is Life. Life is everywhere, Life is all things. Life is never separate from itself. Life never dies. There is only *Life*.

However, we humans have a talent that we share with other creatures of the Earth: the ability to limit our own 'aliveness'. When we are subjected to certain stresses, particularly in childhood and around the time of birth, we shut down our own energy flows out of fear and to make life tolerable. Almost every human being does this to some degree.

The process of *living* then, becomes one of reconnecting ourselves to Life, of resolving the issues that caused us to separate ourselves from Life in the first place. Life exists at many levels, so there are many ways of going about this.

The purpose of this book is to share more of my experience with you. I cannot create the experience for you in a book, but I can help you to see your life in a new light.

A book is food for the mind – yet the final realisation of Unity occurs in the heart. Our barriers to Unity are kept in place mainly by the mind, even though they are equally experiences of the body. It is only through conscious effort and decision acting through the mind that our barriers can be unlocked and released, to return to the Cosmos. They have served their purpose – in our world of polarities, you often know a thing best when you have known its opposite. How bright the faintest glimmer of light in a dark room. How bright the faintest glimmer of Light in a darkened heart.

The gift of the Universe that makes us uniquely human, and one which sets us apart from all other creatures of the Earth, is our ability to recognise patterns. You are doing it right now. Language, reading and writing, are all about recognising patterns – the patterns of sounds and symbols.

No other creatures of the Earth can do this to anywhere near the degree of accuracy that we can. Our nearest cousins, the chimpanzees, and a few other apes have a tiny amount of this ability – a fraction of a percent of our own. This is due to the construction of our brains. Our own evolution has been directly connected to it, and our ability to perceive our own higher consciousness and follow its direction is part of its gift.

Since everything that occurs both on the Earth and in the Cosmos is rhythmic by nature, so too are our own lives. Our ability to analyse the patterns and rhythms in our own lives gives us another unique ability: *choice*.

To choose to follow our own natural rhythms – or to avoid them. We are the only creature of the Earth who can make this choice. We alone can disregard our innate, inner nature. We often do so out of ignorance, believing something is a certain way, and following it even if it hurts. Our own psychology is often at odds with our own best interests.

However, as we begin to notice the patterns around us,

the cycles and rhythms of life, we can also begin to experience our own cycles and rhythms, to use them rather than to oppose them, and ultimately, to re-experience our own Unity with all Creation.

One of the most powerful memories of my Unity experience was the feeling of billions of arms throughout the Universe reaching upward – all reaching for Unity, for Reunion with their own Source. I felt the great swirling Dance that is the Cosmos, all under the watchful senses of the Great Choreographer. There was no feeling of randomness, but a deep awareness of interweaving strands of energy, of everything in motion, and yet all an integral part of an even greater motion – the expanding Universe. Underlying it all, there was an overwhelming sense of Purpose.

This is no fickle, haphazard Universe we are part of – it is going *somewhere*. And *we*, the human race, are a vital part of its journey.

The terms 'cycles' and 'rhythms' should be explained as they are used in this book. Cycle literally means 'circle'. Not necessarily a circle as in geometry, but rather as an event that begins in one place and winds up back in the same place. An example in nature of a cyclic event is the evaporation cycle:

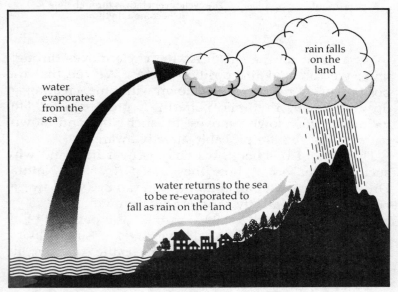

rain falls on the land

water evaporates from the sea

water returns to the sea to be re-evaporated to fall as rain on the land

THE PULSE OF LIFE

Water evaporates from the sea or land, condenses high in the atmosphere, and falls back to Earth as rain, to be re-evaporated and so on. This is a cyclic event, but not a rhythmic event, because each cycle does not occur regularly over a period of time. There is an overall periodic rainfall pattern, as we shall see later, but each single rainfall does not happen at a regular time interval.

A rhythmic event is also cyclic, but each cycle occurs over the same time interval. An example is the movement of the Earth around the Sun. The physical movement is a circle (or almost a circle), and the Earth returns physically to the same position relative to the Sun each 365¼ days, completing a cycle. However, the cycle is also a rhythm because it occurs at regular time intervals.

We can illustrate how a cycle becomes a rhythm in the following figure:

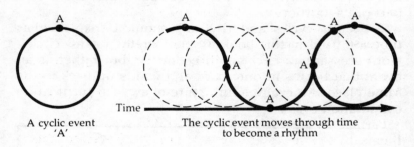

A cyclic event
'A'

Time

The cyclic event moves through time
to become a rhythm

'A' is a point on the circle. As the circle moves through time, we can plot the position of 'A'. We see that the position of 'A' moves up and down with time, creating an up and down, rhythmic pattern. A great deal of life, including your own, moves in such 'up and down' patterns, as you are probably already aware!

Throughout this book, we will discover how and why such patterns occur, how they are part of the Natural Order of your own life, and how you can use your awareness of them creatively for your own growth.

The Universe itself establishes the basic patterns of all that dwell within it. The Universe is a single living organism, and the life of the Universe is the collective life of all within it. As the Universe lives, so all within it live, and vice versa.

THE RHYTHMS OF THE UNIVERSE

When it began, the Universe established its own creative pattern – *Expansion and Contraction* – one of the basic processes of the Universe.

Expanding from a single ball of energy the size of a pea, the Universe has now grown to a being of almost unimaginable size and the evidence is that it will get a great deal larger before it contracts back into itself, to be reborn in another 'Big Bang' through rebound.

Thinking about the patterns of our own lives, don't we experience going into ourselves deeply as a sort of inner collapse? We feel heavy, dense, immobile. We are having a 'dark night of the soul'. And isn't this always followed by a period of expansion, to come more out of ourselves into the world?

In the Universe, the first contraction following the Great Expansion (the Big Bang), was the contraction of energy into the elementary particles which later contracted further to create atoms. This key movement of *Energy into Matter* was the setting into motion of several other Universal processes, for example, Evolution. We tend to think of this word only in connection with the organic kingdoms, but the mineral kingdom, the first kingdom, has also evolved. Minerals evolve not through procreation, but through re-creation.

Particles re-create themselves into atoms. Atoms re-create themselves into molecules. Molecules re-create themselves into minerals. And minerals, ultimately, re-create themselves into planets, where the cycle begins again.

The re-creation of the mineral kingdom (and I include herein all that is not plant or animal), involves another fundamental process of the Universe: *Birth – Life – Death – Rebirth*. The Universe continually recycles its energies and its matter.

In the beginning, the newly forming atoms were almost all hydrogen, with a small scattering of helium. The physical Universe began then, as a diffuse cloud of gas.

At this early birth stage the Universe was several thousand times hotter than the Sun, but as it continued to expand, it also cooled. Probably due to uneven cooling, the hydrogen began to separate and concentrate in smaller, slightly more compact clouds. Gravity (a relatively weak force) began to draw gas into the centre of each cloud, and as the flow to the centre began, the clouds started to rotate, setting up whirls and eddies.

It was the beginning of the next basic pattern of the Universe – the *Movement of Matter into Density*.

As more and more gas was gathered in, hot spots began to develop in the centres of the eddies, as the gas began to compact and heat up. As the compaction continued, the gravity increased, drawing in yet more gas, to provide yet more compaction and heat, to draw in yet more gas, and so on.

On and on until the gas at the very centre became so hot, that the atoms of gas began to stick together or fuse. The fusion of hydrogen atoms to create helium released light particles that were bound up in the structure of the atoms.

The light of the first stars, then began to fill the Universe. Light is born of stars – light that was locked up in the elementary particles at the birth of the Universe. Light that is an expansion from the centres of stars even as their centres move into greater contraction. And in the centres of stars, the last of the five Universal patterns begins: the *Movement into Complexity*.

As the hydrogen fuses to form helium, releasing light, heat is also released, causing the centres to become even hotter. At higher temperatures and pressures, helium begins to fuse to form more complex atoms. This fusion releases yet more heat and light, to provide even more fusion, into even more complex atoms.

So, in the birth process of a star, hydrogen is drawn by gravity to a collapsing and fusing centre, where the Life process takes place: the fusion of gas into more complex atoms – heavy atoms, such as silicon, oxygen, and iron and many others. A star creates as a by-product of its own life, heavy elements – which at a later stage, form minerals, and ultimately, men.

Like all things that live in the Universe, stars die. Hydrogen-rich stars explode (expand) as they die, scattering their core of heavy elements and their remaining hydrogen back into the broth of the Universe. Hydrogen-poor stars collapse inward on themselves (contract), to become white dwarves, to collapse yet again to become neutron stars, perhaps to collapse yet again to become black holes.

THE RHYTHMS OF THE UNIVERSE

To become matter so dense that it begins to approximate the original density before the Big Bang.

The pattern of rhythm and vibration is imbedded in the atoms themselves. Atoms and molecules (groups of atoms) all vibrate – they are in constant motion. Forces of attraction and repulsion are at work even at the subatomic level, creating a series of relationships between particles that are, in their own way, not unlike certain human relationships. Perhaps you have noticed the pattern in a close relationship of your own – you will let someone just so close, and then it is necessary to pull away slightly, then to come close again, only to pull away once more.

In a recent article, a noted atomic physicist described the inner portion of the atom, the nucleus, thus:

> It seems that the nucleus sometimes acts like an elastic solid, sometimes like a liquid, and sometimes like silly putty. It can quiver, ring or oscillate.[1]

Each element has its own series of energy relationships, and when an atom is disturbed by a certain type of magnetic field, its components resonate in a characteristic way. This resonance can be measured, and as each element resonates in its own distinct way, it is a useful tool for analysing what a particular substance is made of. The resonance has a lot to do with the atoms' electrons, and the analytic technique is called Electron Spin Resonance.

Vibration in matter also depends on the type of matter. In gases, there is a great deal of vibration, although it tends to have very little rhythm to it. The individual atoms of the gas are vibrating, but they are relatively far apart, and each atom moves more or less as an individual, and at random.

In liquids, the atoms are closer together, and tend to interact with each other. Rhythm in water, for example wave motions, are produced by energy transmitted from one atom to the next, causing them to move in a distinct pattern.

In solids, atoms not only vibrate, but they vibrate in a very fixed pattern with regard to each other. Although in gases and liquids, atoms are fairly free to move about, in a solid they are locked into a rigid pattern relative to one another. This is why gases and liquids flow – because their atoms are not locked into one another. The process of freezing gases or liquids is to lower their rate of vibration until their atoms literally 'freeze' in position.

Discharging the energy of vibration through heat and light is how stars create heavy elements, elements with a lower vibratory rate than the lighter elements from which they were created.

In the beginning, and even now, for the Universe is a relatively young place, the majority of stars were hydrogen-rich. As these stars die and scatter, their remaining hydrogen mixes with that of other dead stars, and new stars are born – a new generation. Stars are constantly being born and reborn. In the autumn and winter sky in the Northern Hemisphere, you can see with your own eyes stars being born.

The Pleiades, for example. Seven stars surrounded by a dimly-lit gas cloud – the cloud from which they are condensing. If you had walked the earth 70,000 years ago (a mere instant in Universal time), there would have been nothing to see. They are that new. The earliest cave-men of Europe were here by that time – so these are stars that are younger than men.

Minerals too are reborn from dying stars. The scattered core of heavy elements forming a dust cloud drawn by gravity to yet living stars, begins its own movement into density and complexity.

Certain atoms are attracted to certain other atoms, and these groups of atoms are attracted to other groups like themselves. The Universal law of 'Like attracts Like' is at work even among atoms, and thus a mineral is born.

As larger and larger grains build up, they begin to be drawn together to form yet larger grains. The grains accumulate into lumps, the lumps into boulders, the boulders into planets. And so, from a cloud of hydrogen gas, a solar system is born. So *our* solar system was born.

Thus, in the birth of the Universe, a series of cycles, rhythms, patterns and relationships were begun that reflect through all levels of creation:

1. Expansion and Contraction
2. Movement of Energy into Matter

3. Birth – Life – Death – Rebirth

4. Movement of Matter into Density

5. Movement into Complexity

In the following chapters we will see how all life, including your own, follows these five basic patterns.

Our galaxy sets the cyclic tone for our immediate part of the Universe, although it in turn is only one of a large cluster of other galaxies. Our galaxy rotates around its central core, and our own star, far out in one of the spiral arms, revolves around the centre once every 200 million years.

It is only one Sun out of several hundred billion in our galaxy alone, which would by any standard be quite unremarkable.

Yet, on one planet of this minor star, in a minor galaxy, one of the Universe's most important experiments is under way.

You.

Chapter 2

THE RHYTHMS OF THE EARTH

A cloud does not know why it moves in just such a direction and at such a speed; It feels an impulse . . . this is the place to go now. But the sky knows the reasons and patterns behind all clouds, and you will know too when you lift yourself high enough to see beyond horizons.

RICHARD BACH
Illusions (1977)

The idea that the natural cycles of the Solar System have some effect on life on the Earth has been around for a long time. Long has man watched the movement of the Sun, Moon and Planets across the sky, and tried to make some sense of it.

Astrology, one of the oldest 'sciences', evolved as an answer to man's hunger to know the future, to make himself more secure by armouring himself against both natural and man-made catastrophies.

Although astrology, when used simply as a fortune-telling device, can be questionable, there are very definite and well-investigated cycles and rhythms in the plant and animal kingdoms that have an absolute correspondence to astronomical movements. We will look specifically at those in later chapters, but for the moment, let's see what those movements actually are.

Solar cycles

The Sun goes through a number of cycles, in addition to its own life – death – rebirth cycle. The Sun is a third generation star; that is, made up from the remains of two other stages of star-death. We know this from studies of the chemical make-up of the Sun, and that it is about half-way through its own 10 thousand million year lifetime.

THE RHYTHMS OF THE EARTH

Recently, there has been speculation that the Sun is half of a double star – that is, two stars moving around each other, like two stones rotating on opposite ends of a piece of twine. The twine in this case being gravity. This wouldn't be too surprising, as stars are born in batches, and somewhere in the galaxy are brothers and sisters of the Sun. It wouldn't be all that improbable that there is still a 'family relationship' maintained by gravity.

It has been suggested that the Sun's 'companion' star returns every 26 million years or so. This cycle would correspond with periodic mass extinctions of plants and especially animals on the Earth. One of the most dramatic of these was about 65 million years ago when the dinosaurs and many, many other species died out suddenly.

It is suggested also that as this 'companion' star – which has been named the 'Death Star' or Nemesis – approaches our Solar System, it brings with it its own Solar System, and a cloud of comets. Our own star has such a comet cloud, hovering outside of Pluto's orbit, that a near approach by Nemesis would send not only its own cloud of comets into a great turmoil, but ours as well. Although such a near miss would not necessarily upset the orbits of the planets, the planet that once existed between Mars and Jupiter may well have been destroyed by a collision with one of the Death Stars own planets, or perhaps even by tidal forces from a near miss. At the very least, it would send a rain of comets throughout the Solar System.

Some of these comets, or perhaps an asteroid or other planetary debris, could easily impact with the Earth, throwing immense dust clouds into the atmosphere, and blotting out the Sun for many months. This is a scenario not unlike the 'Nuclear Winter', where clouds of smoke and dust from a surprisingly small number of nuclear explosions could reduce sunlight to such a degree that a winter of several years duration could engulf the entire planet.

This comet rain may not have always been a disaster, however, as it has been speculated that organic life may have been spread through the Universe by just such comet encounters.

In the body of the Sun itself, the fusion process already described takes place, but at its surface disturbances occur that have a more direct connection with Earth life – *sunspots*.

Sunspots are abrupt gas explosions, which launch ionic effects into space that are felt here on Earth. These effects show in the atmospheric electricity of our planet, fade out radio reception and cause geomagnetic storms. It could even be said that we live within the 'atmosphere' of the sun.

There are two distinct sunspot cycles – 11 years and 40 years. Our evidence for these cycles goes back 500 million years. The growth of plants is very much connected with the sunspot cycle, and tree ring measurements confirm this. Likewise, the amount of organic debris washing into lakes and ponds also varies with the cycle. Every year, a thin layer of silt, called a varve, is deposited. If the deposits which have accumulated over many years are studied – as can sometimes occur when ancient lakebeds have been turned to stone and later exposed – the varying thickness of the varves shows a definite 11 year cycle.

Modern records show that the water level of Lake Victoria-Nyanza changes in accordance with the rhythm of sunspots, as well as the numbers of icebergs in the Atlantic Ocean. Studies have shown a definite correlation between sunspot cycles and rainfall, again an 11 year cycle. There are also shorter cycles of rainfall that are connected with other Cosmic events; the moon's phase being significant in the shorter term, as we will see later in the chapter.

It has even been noticed that wine production is very much a cyclical process, and related to the 11 year sunspot cycle. Humans, of course, are also affected by this cycle.

Another major effect on the Earth of sunspots is a disturbance of the Earth's magnetic field. There are a number of biological effects that relate to this, which will be discussed in later chapters, but there is also the effect on the planetary body of the Earth itself.

A French geophysicist, Pierre Bernard, built extremely sensitive instruments called seismographs to measure very faint tremors in the Earth's crust. Once again, an 11 year cycle appeared. Years in which micro-seismic tremors are most intense are those in which there is a sharp decline in solar activity.[1]

The Sun emits a broad range of light rays and radiations, many of which are variable and unpredictable. The vagaries of the Sun are not without consequence to the Earth – the length of a day on Earth can even be altered as a result. It is only by a fraction of a second, but think of the enormous energy required to achieve this. It is actually rather an ordinary occurrence, but it has only been noticed since the invention of super-accurate atomic clocks. There is even some evidence that gravity is affected to a small degree.

Another solar effect, which was noted from quite an unusual source, appears on a seasonal basis. A few years ago in England a group was investigating the energy of stone circles, by both scientific and psychic means. In the vicinity of the Rollright Stones in Oxfordshire, a device was being operated for picking up microsounds. In passing the stones, a series of clicks was heard that were assumed to be either background noise or machine noise. It was soon noticed that these were only heard when near the stones, and a pattern was established with maximum emissions at sunrise, declining throughout the day.

A seasonal pattern was also discovered, with peaks and troughs at the times of the solstices and equinoxes. It is possible that the machine was just hearing the varied minerals of the stones expanding unevenly in the sun, but even if this was the case, imagine the unheard symphony going on around us all the time, keeping beat to the seasons.

Lunar cycles

Almost everyone is aware that the ocean tides are caused by the movement of the Moon. But the belief that the Moon plays a part in controlling the weather, although as old as the Chaldeans, is almost unknown today. Yet a study done in 1962 found a direct correlation between widespread rainfall and the phases of the Moon in the USA. Another study in Australia produced similar results.

The probable mechanism itself wasn't discovered until 1963 when the IMP-1 satellite noticed that the 'solar wind', the stream of particles from the Sun, was stopped and deflected when the Moon was in a certain position to the

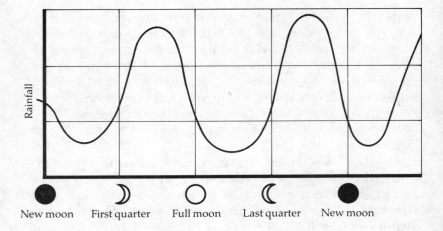

New moon   First quarter   Full moon   Last quarter   New moon

Sun. The particles thus hit the Earth differently or not at all. Meteoric dust would be similarly affected.

The Earth receives a continuous fall of dust from space – enough to result in almost a third of the diameter of the Earth having been built up by it over the past 500 million years or so. The solar wind greatly affects this dustfall.

Meteoric dust has been shown to condense water vapour in clouds, causing rain. Thus, the phase (or position) of the Moon will to some extent regulate meteoric dustfall, thus regulating rainfall.[2]

As instrumentation has improved in recent years, it has been discovered that the land also has a 'tide'. Measurements of 3 to 4 inches have been recorded, where the land surface actually moves up and down like the tides of the ocean.

Solar–Lunar

The Sun-Moon eclipses which occur roughly every 18½ years, always occur at the same point in the sky. This 18½ year cycle has been identified in the records of the tides of the Nile (going back 4000 years), as well as in the 11 year sunspot cycle. The Chaldeans knew this period, and named it Saros.

The Saros cycle has not been especially noted in the other kingdoms, but its time period correlates curiously well with certain human psychological cycles (see chapter 5).

Long term weather cycles have been identified by Dr Raymond Wheeler of the University of Kansas. Every 100 years there is a serious decline in rainfall world-wide, combined with a fall in temperature. He also identifies a 170 year and 510 year cycle. How these cycles profoundly influence human society is seen in chapter 8.

Interior geologic cycles

The inner cycles of the Earth itself are well enough known, but we don't yet know whether there is a rhythm to them. We can well assume that if the 'Death Star' hypothesis is correct, there will no doubt be some sort of long term rhythm connected with them.

We do know that the planet has gone through a series of ice ages – technically we are still in one now, or at least at its end. We have evidence that there have been ice ages periodically for at least the past 200 million years, and probably longer than that. Exactly why this is the case, is still anyone's guess. The position of the Earth relative to the 'Death Star' passing, however, could be one possible cause, although the last series of ice ages has had a much shorter time span than the last supposed passing of the 'Death Star'.

We also know that the mineral matter of the Earth re-cycles itself more or less continually. Heat from the interior, produced by radioactive decay, causes convection currents to form in the almost molten interior. Hotter material from deeper within the Earth rises, and cooler, denser material sinks. This is the mechanism that propels the continents in their wandering, and which has been going on for at least 200 million years. The full process is described in my book *The Cosmic Crystal Spiral*, and is presented on the following page in an abbreviated form.

In this figure hot material is rising in the middle of the Atlantic Ocean, forming the Mid-Atlantic Ridge. As this material rises and cools, it forces apart the outer shell of the Earth, called the crust, which makes up the ocean floor and the continents. On the opposite sides of the conti-

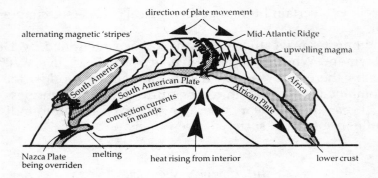

nents, crust material is being pulled back under and re-melted, to rise yet again, to be drawn under yet again, and so on.

In this manner, the Earth constantly revitalises and renews itself. Whether or not this revitalising follows a regular cycle in time is unknown, but if the Sun does indeed have a 'companion' star that returns every 26 million years or so, then we might well speculate on this as a trigger for much of the Earth's larger scale activity.

We know that 200 to 300 million years ago, the continents were all part of one landmass, a supercontinent called Pangaea, which broke up and began to drift apart, to form the current continents.

Why did this happen in the first place?

I have a strong intuition that there is a connection between the continental break-up and the planet formerly occupying the orbit between Mars and Jupiter, where we now find the asteroid belt. Should our Solar System have had a 'near miss' with the Solar System of the 'Death Star', that is, should the planetary alignments have been critical, vast tidal forces between planets could have been enough to trigger both the break-up of the asteroid planet, and continental movements on our own.

It is possible of course, that the continents have *always* moved, and that Pangaea was simply a place where they were all lumped together briefly before continuing their wandering.

Either case, I believe, presents a fascinating picture of our own living planet.

Chapter 3

THE RHYTHMS OF THE PLANT AND ANIMAL KINGDOMS

Heard melodies are sweet, but those unheard are sweeter.

JOHN KEATS
Ode on a Grecian Urn (1820)

In the last chapters we looked at the basic cosmic and planetary rhythms. Let us now look at the plant and animal kingdoms, and see how these rhythms manifest.

Organic life is absolutely dependent on and regulated by rhythm – the basic processes of individual cells, of plants and even their constituent atoms, as well as the larger rhythms of individual body organs. In our own bodies we experience the familiar rhythms of heartbeat and breathing, and there are dozens of others of which we are only faintly aware, if at all.

Many of the basic rhythms are those set by the Cosmos, especially the Sun and Moon. The most obvious rhythms are the daily, lunar, monthly and yearly rhythms, and examples abound of each.

Scientists have long believed that *all* solar and lunar factors are simple and obvious, for example, the intensity of sunlight or moonlight, or the humidity, temperature and strength of the tides controlling the reproductive cycles of plants and animals. In most cases tested there have indeed been regulating mechanisms connected to natural cosmic cycles, but many do not fall into known or obvious categories.

Bunning showed that if dry grain seed is kept in a container at constant temperature, the percentage of seed taken from the container that will germinate depends on the season of the year. Dry seed kept at low temperature is almost lifeless. How could the seed be aware of what part of the year it is taken from the container?[1]

Other startling evidence of subtle, and as yet unknown influences appeared in a unique experiment by Professor Brown of Northwestern University, USA.

He had live oysters sent in closed, darkened containers from Long Island Sound to his laboratory at Evanston, Illinois – a thousand miles inland. When they arrived, he measured their activity by noting the opening and closing of their valves. They kept to their natural rhythms at first, the rhythm of the tides in Long Island Sound.

However, within 15 days they adopted a new rhythm – the oysters now opened at the time the tide would have flooded Evanston, had the town been on the seashore! The oysters had abandoned their natural rhythm to actual tides, and had reverted to a purely lunar rhythm – the time when the Moon passed overhead at Evanston.[2]

How did they know?

Brown next experimented with rats, and discovered that they too respond to the movements of the Moon. Rats kept in cages with constant conditions, and constant light, were shown to be more active during the hours the Moon was below the horizon, and quietest when it was above the horizon.

Again, how did they know?

According to Brown, the organisms have a timing mechanism that is actually sensitive to changes in the subtle rhythms of the Earth itself.[3] Humans also demonstrate this acute sensitivity, as we shall later discover.

The Sun exerts a direct and obvious influence – plants open or close leaves or flowers in direct response to sunlight or the lack of it. A few flowers are so sensitive to light changes that they will close even at the approach of a shadow.

Animals sleep, hunt and feed by daylight or darkness. These processes are well known, and are directly related to the presence or absence of sunlight. Likewise, seasonal changes also due to the amount and intensity of sunlight, are well known.

Combined rhythms

There are other rhythms too, which are not obviously

connected to astronomical movement, but are probably combined rhythms of the Sun, Moon and Earth itself.

In plants, especially those collected for medicinal purposes, it has been noticed that their potencies are constantly changing, often in relationship to the Moon. A cancer research institute in Switzerland found in its study of mistletoe '. . . that the properties of the plant were drastically affected not only by local time and weather conditions, but by . . . the phases of the moon and the occurrence of an eclipse'.[4]

The classic example among animals is lemmings. Every 3.86 years, there is a stirring in the lemming population. There are radical hormone changes and their circulatory system becomes saturated with steroids – up to thirty times the normal. Then their march begins – a wild and frenzied stampede towards the sea – and then straight into it. By some unknown process, a few remain on shore, a natural selection to provide a nucleus for a new lemming population. (I often wonder if the urge to make war in humans may not have a lemming-like urge for population control.)

There is a 9.6 year cycle in the population of Canadian snowshoe rabbits. The life cycles of the lynx, marten, fishers, owls and hawks also average 9.6 years.[5] And every 22.7 years, there is a high and a low cycle in the partridge population. This could be related to the 11.2 year sunspot cycle.

Much of our natural rhythm, both for ourselves and the plant and animal kingdoms, may be tied to the internal rhythms of the Earth itself. The natural pulses in the Earth's own magnetic and electric fields, pulsing between 1 and 30 Hz, and fluctuating every 24 hours, appear to set the internal clocks of most, if not all, organisms.

These rhythms appear to affect hormone secretions in animals (and in humans) that, amongst other things, regulate sleep. In experiments, it has been shown that animal behaviour can be highly modified simply by changing the frequency of weak electromagnetic fields. These fields appear to alter brain-wave function, and animals can be sent into a deep sleep or into a frenzy just by moving the frequency up and down.[6]

Maintaining rhythm is essential to survival for all organisms. Loss of rhythm in one part of an organism which is not quickly regained, can upset the life processes of the entire organism. Experiments have shown that artificially imposed rhythms, out of synchronisation with the natural rhythm of an organism, is usually fatal.

In a classic experiment, regulatory glands from cockroaches set to normal daytime were transplanted into other cockroaches, who were also on normal daytime – they all remained healthy. When regulatory glands from cockroaches, whose day-night cycle was reversed, were transplanted into normal cockroaches, the host cockroaches all died of intestinal cancer.[7]

Plants too have shown themselves to be extremely sensitive to rhythm. In her book *The Sound of Music and Plants*, Dorothy Retallack recounts experiments in which she played various sorts of music to plants. She discovered that classic and pop-classic music stimulated plant growth, and created hearty plants with lush foliage. Plants played this music tended to grow toward the music source.

Rock music on the other hand, created plants growing in bizarre and grotesque shapes, and which soon died. These plants tried to escape the music by growing away from the music source. In her experiments a number of different types of plants all responded in the same way. Other researchers have also shown that random noise can retard the growth of plants by as much as 40 percent.

Plants and animals are highly sensitive in ways that are outside the usual areas of sensitivity to solar and lunar influences. For example, a researcher was trying to trace the movement of roots on a smoked glass surface, placed in such a way that as the root tip moved over the surface, it would leave a trace. He noticed that with certain kinds of beans and peas, it was impossible. In most cases, just before the tip of the root reached the surface, it would stop growing, refusing to push downward onto the impenetrable glass. Somehow, the root tips knew the glass was there.

In a similar way climbing plants can sense supports. In one experiment, a stick was placed near a young pea plant, and within the next few hours the tendrils had begun to move towards it. Eventually, the whole plant leaned towards the support as the tendril began to grasp it. Somehow the plant knew the support was there!

A D Semenenko demonstrated that plants do have memory, and proposes that plants selectively absorb and retain useful information, and actively search for needed information. There is evidence that this is a rhythmic phenomenon, with about one complete circuit per day.[8] In his experiments, a number of both wild and cultivated plants were subjected to flashes of light at fixed intervals, and the response of the plant measured, particularly leaf motion. When the light was due, but not flashed, the plants began to move in the direction of the light, in anticipation of the light – as if 'looking' for it.

Such extreme sensitivity is also shown even at the less complex levels of the animal kingdom. An example is the bean aphid, which can either give birth to live offspring or lay eggs, depending on the time of the year and the length of the day. When daylight lasts longer than fourteen hours and fifty-five minutes, the offspring is born alive. If the day is even a few minutes shorter, the offspring is born inside an egg that will hatch later. Somewhere in the female bean aphid's body is a *very* finely tuned mechanism.

There has been a long tradition that sacred dances generate an energy that could be picked up by plants. A fascinating experiment was performed by Dr Singh carrying on the work of Sir Jagadis Bose. An assistant performed an Indian sacred dance daily for a batch of marigolds. These plants grew 60 percent taller than the control marigolds in a 'un-danced' batch. Dr Singh believes that the plants were responding to the rhythms of the dance transmitted through the ground.[9]

Very often in nature, where a strong rhythm is not present, the creatures involved create one for themselves! It's as if nature abhors a long silence. Whatever sound-making device is available, creatures of all sorts do a great deal of 'gabbling'. It is as if social conversation is necessary for survival at all levels of creation. It was found on experiments with rats, that those who had stimulus through handling or other contact developed less illness. It was also found that electric shocks had exactly the same benefit as kind handling!

We know that this is true in humans as well. Stimulus is absolutely necessary for survival – a baby left unheld, uncared for is likely to die. Throughout our lives we try to re-create the constant stimulus of the womb, but we create substitutes that provide the necessary stimuli. We know now in psychology that if children don't get positive stim-ulus, they will do whatever necessary to get negative stimulus, which is better than nothing!

In transactional analysis, stimulus in humans, which most often comes from non-physical contact, is called 'stroking'. In humans, we do it at cocktail parties, in everyday gossip, or on the telephone with friends.

Termites make sounds to each other by beating their heads against the floor of their nests. There is a high degree of organisation in the drumming; the beats are in regular, rhythmic phrases.[10]

Other animals use other methods. Drumming with the feet is done by prairie hens, rabbits and mice – the head is banged by woodpeckers and several other birds. Fish make sounds by clicking their teeth, blowing air, and drumming muscles against inflated air bladders.

Gorillas beat their chests. Animals with loose skeletons rattle them. Toads sing to one another. Even earthworms make sounds – faint stacatto notes in regular clusters.[11]

Young chimpanzees explore the possibilities of thump-ing, foot-stamping and clapping. Adult chimps develop organised social drumming sessions, often lasting a half-hour or more. One animal after another stamps, screams and beats on tree-stumps or hollow logs.[12] It appears to be a form of community-building activity, getting all of the members 'in tune' with each other.

Humans make music.

We are all tuned to the same pulse of life, regardless of what kingdom we are part of. Perhaps this is truly the 'Music of the Spheres'.

Thomas says:

> The recorded sounds of the humpback whale . . . can be listened to as a part of music, like an isolated section of an orchestra. If we had better hearing, the rhythmic tympari of schools of mollusks, or even the distant harmonics of midges hanging over meadows in the sun, the combined sound might lift us off our feet.[13]

There is even grounds in physics to suggest that rhythm is

part of the biological memory of Creation in all living organisms. Morowitz presents the case in thermodynamic terms; that the flow of energy onto the Earth from the Sun is mathematically destined to bring matter into an increasingly ordered state of being. [14]

The result is molecules of higher and higher complexity, with the emergence of cycles for the storage and release of energy.

Rhythm in biology may well be the earliest memory – a score for the transformation of inanimate matter in chaos, into the order of living forms.

In Backster's work with plants, and even in scrapings from human tissue, polygraphs connected to even minute bits of living tissue produced the same results – they responded to outside stimuli in exactly the same way as whole plants. Perception seems to take place at a cellular level. [15] Certainly cells are likely to retain the sensory structures that would have evolved to preserve the first single-celled creatures.

Even the human body retains these sensory devices (whatever they may be). In bioenergetics, the whole process is involved in unlocking cellular memory of past traumatic events, which causes the muscles to 'freeze'. The 'freezing' may be nothing more than saturating cellular systems with the chemicals of unexpressed emotional events – emotions are chemical events in the body.

It has been found that by using certain techniques of body posture there is a release of these 'locked up' emotions, a cathartic release takes place, and afterwards the body may actually change shape, as muscles begin to move more freely.

The subtle mechanism by which various organisms are interconnected are only gradually becoming known. Indeed, the word 'psychic' seems to describe best what is presently known. But as our understanding of the energies that surround us grows, we will doubtless find a perfectly explainable (although no less mysterious) mechanism. And as our knowledge grows deeper, we will doubtless see how the rhythm of life sets the tone for all interactions between the kingdoms.

Some of the pioneering scientific discoveries about interactions were made by Cleve Backster. On a purely whimsical thought he decided to hook a polygraph (lie detector) up to a plant in his office. After a while he noticed something fascinating – the plant was showing a tracing almost identical to that shown by humans 'experiencing somewhat mild emotional stimulation'.

His next step was to see if the plant would show a similar response to humans experiencing fear and anxiety – an immediate polygraph response. What he discovered was startling – he had only to *think* about burning the leaf with the electrode attached and the polygraph leapt into action – showing a pattern of 'anxiety'.

Backster later discovered that plants respond immediately when certain people enter the room, and even showed a severe 'anxiety' reaction when one person whose job involved roasting plants entered the room. He also demonstrated that plants can pick up anxiety from animals, even if they are in another room.[16]

Other experiments and experimenters have shown that plants can respond to the thoughts of their owners at almost unlimited distances.

Dr Victor Adamenko, a Soviet physicist, also observes that plants can receive communication at a distance of hundreds of miles. He has found that metallic containers and Faraday screens have no effect in stopping the communications. He believes that whatever energies are involved, they must fall outside the known electromagnetic spectrum.[17] It has even been observed that in polygraph tracings, plants tune into their masters by matching beat-for-beat the pulsating heart of their owners.[18]

The Pipiles in Central America refrain from intercourse four days before the sowing of seeds. Then they believe that by making love just before the seeds are planted, the fertility of the fields is increased.[19]

This may not be as odd as it sounds. In other polygraph experiments, plants were placed with groups of students talking about various subjects. When dull subjects such as engineering were being discussed, the tracings showed little activity. But when sex was discussed, the tracings became quite active![20]

Plants are also sensitive to animals, as demonstrated in some experiments done by Backster. A device was constructed to immerse live brine shrimp (mostly used as tropical fish food), into a container of boiling water at random intervals. As a control, the machine would also randomly immerse water with no shrimp into boiling water.

The experiment was done with no one in the building to send any thoughts to the three philodendron plants in separate rooms, each hooked up to its own polygraph. Each of the three showed acute stress symptoms each time the shrimp were immersed, and no reaction when only water was immersed. Clearly, they were responding to the distress of the dying shrimp.

Plants were even shown to have a sensitivity to minerals. Adamenko trained plants to respond in the presence of a specific mineral, and in a significant number of experiments, they did just that.[21]

Recent experiments by a doctor in Australia have shown that the growth of salt crystals can be influenced by human thought, and that the crystals communicated their new growth patterns to each other. He has also shown that the transmitted patterns of growth follow a rhythmic wave-pattern.

What underlies all of these responses?

Albert Szenet-Gyorgi, a Nobel Prize winner, believes that emotional states may generate a yet unknown type of subatomic energy, one that passes unhindered through 'normal' matter. We know that such particles exist: the neutrino, generated in the solar fusion process, is so small that it passes right through the Earth without hitting anything. Several billion of them have passed through your body while you were reading this sentence. It is not suggested, by the way, that these particles being generated *are* neutrinos, but as emotions are electrochemical body events generating a great deal of energy, the release of subatomic particles as a by-product is not too unlikely.

All of this may seem a bit removed from the immediate subject of rhythms and cycles, but it is to underline that there are subtle energies at work around us and as part of us every second – most of which we are unaware – that rhythmically shape our lives and the lives of everything that surrounds us.

Robert Prinable of the Bellin Partnership, once gave the most intuitively accurate definition I have ever heard of

the word *life*: 'Life is the flow of energy through structure'.
I have a feeling that it could be slightly altered to say:

'Life is the *pulse* of energy through structure'.

Chapter 4

BODY RHYTHMS

Nor is it a new thing for man to invent an existence
that he imagines to be above the rest of nature; . . .
As illusion, it has never worked out . . . Man is
embedded in nature.

LEWIS THOMAS
The Lives of A Cell (1974)

We have looked at natural cycles and rhythms which
connect the other kingdoms to the Cosmos, to the Earth,
and to each other. The Kingdom of Man is likewise connected by his biology to the rhythms of nature.

Even in our physical development, we reproduce the
evolutionary pattern of our kingdom: we begin as a single
cell, then a colony of cells, then an embryo like a fish, an
amphibian, and finally a mammal.

At one stage during the development of the embryo,
human, bird, pig and tortoise embryos are almost identical – and each embryo begins with an urge for Union.

Our sensitivity is as finely tuned as the oyster or the
bean aphid. Our cells dance to the same tune as the
termites. Like the coyote, we find our own way to howl at
the Full Moon, and our faces change with the seasons, like
the forests and fields. Lewis Thomas, in *Lives of a Cell*,
underlines our sensitivity very clearly:

Man comes on as a stupendous lethal force, and the earth
is pictured as something delicate, like rising bubbles at the
surface of a country pond . . .
But it is an illusion to think that there is anything fragile
about the life of the earth; surely this is the toughest
membrane imaginable in the Universe . . . *We* are the
delicate pond . . .[1]

We are sensitive to a large number of influences, most of

them, as with the other kingdoms, rooted in the Cosmos. Like many other creatures, we seem to be very sensitive to changes in the Earth's magnetism. These changes are usually brought about by sunspot activity and certain illnesses show definite peaks that relate to the sunspot cycle.

One of the most startling early discoveries was that the clotting rate of blood varies directly with both sunrise, and with the appearance of sunspots. A Japanese physician, Maki Takata, discovered that the rate of clotting (called the floculation index) varied throughout the day, becoming very low at night, and suddenly rising rapidly at the coming of day. The rise actually begins before sunrise, as if the blood 'knows' that sunrise is coming.

To test that it is something emitted by the sun that the blood is sensing, several people were taken to places where a full eclipse of the sun was to take place. Sure enough, as the eclipse progressed, the floculation index began to drop, rising again just as the eclipse ended. The moon had blocked out whatever solar energy the blood was responding to.

It is still unknown precisely which solar radiation produces the effect, but it is powerful enough to penetrate almost everything except the moon. The effect has been observed everywhere, except one test that was done 600 feet underground in a mine![2]

There is one other solar influence on the blood. Soviet scientists have discovered a direct connection between the number of lymphocytes (a type of white blood cell), and the frequency of sunspots.[3]

In February 1956, there was a series of great solar eruptions. Blood analyses throughout the Soviet Union showed an abnormally low level of certain white blood cells during that month, returning to normal one month later.[4]

Cardiovascular ailments have been likewise shown to increase during periods of intense solar activity.[5]

Other studies show a connection between sunspot activity and the number of traffic accidents, the number of admissions to psychiatric hospitals, suicides, and deaths from bloodclots obstructing the coronary artery.

What is happening exactly?

Two suggestions are made, both of which underline the extreme sensitivity of human beings to the energies of the world around us: sensitivity first, to long-wave radiation, and secondly to the disturbance of the earth's magnetic field.

We are only just beginning to understand the effect of electromagnetic fields on the human body. The first concrete discoveries were made in 1952 by a German scientist, Professor W O Schumann, who identified waves of very low frequency associated with the Earth's own magnetic and electrical field.

Professor Schumann suggested that these waves may influence all life. Important evidence came from some of the first manned space flights – flights at a distance from the Earth where the wave effects are very much reduced. Astronauts returned feeling distressed and disoriented – until devices for generating Schumann waves were installed in spacecrafts.

Schumann waves pulse almost within the same frequency as brain waves – between 1 and 30 Hz. By influencing levels of hormone secretion, patterns of sleep, menstrual cycles, and so on can be affected.

Jet lag may be a result of being shielded by the plane's metallic casing, and flying at an altitude where Schumann waves are considerably weaker than normal. It is usually made worse by moving to a place where the waves are pulsing at a different point in their 24 hour rhythm. Stewardesses on long-haul duty often experience irregular periods, and may stop menstruating altogether.[6] It has been suggested that placing a small magnet on the forehead for a few minutes at the journey's end aids in a more rapid re-orientation. It is also interesting that this is the location on the brain that recent research has shown to be the co-ordinating centre for all brain function.

The effects of man-made electrical and magnetic fields on human health is just beginning to be understood. The Soviet Union has been a pioneer in this field.

If the police radio can influence telephones; if a microwave oven can wipe out information stored in a computer in the same house; is it really surprising that the human body, much of it electrically powered, can likewise be affected?

Professor David Melville has demonstrated that cell membranes exposed to electromagnetic fields stiffen; other doctors are using precisely controlled frequencies to treat allergies – which may in themselves be a result of electro-magnetic pollution.

Dr Jean Munro at the Lister Hospital in London recently presented a paper about a number of patients with a range of complaints: weakness, lethargy, depression, fatigue, colitis and migraine – all brought on by things such as power lines, television sets, computers, cookers, fridges – even light bulbs. The problem frequencies were in the range from 50–60 Hz to 6–8 mega Hz. Other patients, however, reversed the process – they were able to influence electrical equipment!

Microwaves are another major source of 'electromagnetic pollution'. These are the frequencies at which cells appear to communicate with each other, so by interfering with inter-cellular communication, a number of diseases may result. Cancer and leukaemia may be one result.

Work with animals suggests that microwaves upset the balance of calcium ions in the brain, create chromosomal damage, and decrease the activity of immune cells. It wouldn't be surprising to find parallels in human bio-chemistry and especially in brain chemistry. It is well known that, among other things, admissions to psychiatric hospitals rocket on days of strong magnetic disturbance.

However, not all of the effects are negative. For ex-ample, weak pulsed magnetic fields have been used since 1979 to treat bone fractures in the USA. Thousands of fractures have been successfully treated since it was demonstrated that weak pulsed fields stimulate bone growth.

There is another major solar effect on the Earth's en-vironment – the ionisation of the air. It has been discovered that in air charged with positive ions, people are likely to feel headaches, discomfort, and general giddiness. The same people breathing air charged with negative ions can feel cheerful, relaxed and on top form.

The concentration of positive and negative ions in the air depends both on solar activity and on the weather situation (which is often a lunar cycle). Negative ions have a tendency to attach themselves to clouds, which remove them from the environment. Thus, when the weather is cloudy, people tend to feel down and depressed.

Air pollution also tends to negate the natural solar cycles of ionisation – particles of exhaust, dust and smoke tend to accumulate positive ions and cause them to sink earthward, thus increasing the concentration of unhealthy ions at the surface.

The effect of the Moon on human behaviour has been noted since ancient times. The word 'lunatic' was coined by the Romans, and was applied in describing epileptics, who were noticed to have more seizures than usual at the time of the Full Moon.

In the sixteenth century, Paracelsus claimed, '. . . that the insane grew worse at the dark of the moon', when the Moon's attraction on the brain was believed to be the strongest. Such beliefs were legalised in eighteenth century England, at which time a distinction was made between 'insane' which designated the chronically and hopelessly psychotic, and 'lunatic' aberrations which were believed to be accelerated only by the Full Moon. Prior to 1808, Bedlam hospital inmates were beaten at certain lunar periods as a 'prophylaxis against violence'.[8]

Police departments have also noted increases in certain types of crimes which seem to correspond with the Full Moon. It is reported that:

> . . . policemen who deal with telephone complaints have always reported that activity – especially crimes against persons – seemed to increase as the night of the Full Moon drew near. People whose anti-social behaviour had psychotic roots – such as arsonists, kleptomaniacs, destructive drivers, and homicidal alcoholics – seemed to go on a rampage as the moon rounded, calming down as the moon waned.[9]

Such connections between the Moon and human behaviour have long been denied by scientists, mostly based on lack of discernable evidence about the mechanisms to create the psychological effects.

As instruments become more sensitive, new information is beginning to appear. It has been discovered that the Earth's magnetic and electrical field changes with the phases of the Moon, and the effects are similar to those of the sunspot cycle, discussed earlier.

THE PULSE OF LIFE

Dr Arnold Lieber, author of *The Lunar Effect*, believes that the Moon has an unbalancing effect on our body fluids and body chemistry, as well as our electromagnetic field. In a reasonably well-balanced person, this has an unsettling effect, resulting in restlessness or discomfort, but in those with biochemical imbalances that lead to violent behaviour, it is enough to push them over the edge.

As an example, manic-depressives who exhibit maniacal behaviour at the Full Moon are found to have an accelerated metabolism during the full-moon time and this has even been found to accelerate beard growth.

In his fascinating book *Cosmic Clocks*, Michael Gauquelin notes the work of Dr L J Ravitz:

> Dr Ravitz has been measuring for some years the differences in electrical potential between the head and chest of mental patients. Such differences were found to change from day to day; they followed a cyclical pattern even in normal subjects. According to Dr Ravitz, the cycles paralleled seasonal and lunar changes. In the fall (autumn) and winter, maximal positivity tends to occur around new moon and maximal negativity around full moon. The effects of the moon seem to be more pronounced on mental patients than on normal persons since the difference in potential is markedly greater for the future.
>
> This pattern did not suggest to Ravitz that the moon affects human behaviour directly, but by modifying the . . . terrestrial electromagnetic forces the moon could precipitate disorders in persons whose mental balance is precarious.[10]

All matter is in motion, as we saw earlier, including the basic matter of the body – its atoms and molecules. It has been found that atoms of hydrogen, contained in all body tissues, align in a certain direction in magnetic fields if tissue is healthy, and in other directions if tissue is diseased. Even our atoms have some sort of 'awareness'.

Protoplasm, the substance of life itself, pulses with rhythmic activity inside its cellular membrane, probably as a result of the vibration of its molecules. Pulsation in red blood cells has also been noted by Reich.[11]

Heart muscle cells show the greatest capacity for rhythm

of all body cells, and each cell seems capable of generating its own rhythm. If a piece of heart muscle is detached and kept in a saline solution, for example, it will continue to expand and contract – evidence that rhythm is a natural condition of life for a heart cell.

These expansion and contraction cycles appear in other muscles as well, and are for the most part involuntary. The cilia, for example, minute, hair-like structures that line the lungs and bronchial tubes beat in unison, producing waves that have been likened to the waving of a wheat field in the wind. Their function is to move foreign particles such as dust and pollen up and out of the bronchial tubes and keep them from settling in the lungs.

The human body thus has its own internal rhythms, which begin at the cell level, or perhaps at an even more subtle level than that.

The body generates its own pulsing field of energy, the aura, which is shown to be directly connected to the body's own life processes. Lowen describes its connection to the level of excitation in the body, the dynamic tension that propels Life.

As an inner excitement occurs, the aura expands and its colour changes. In depression and pain, the field decreases as blood is withdrawn from the surface of the body.

The aura pulsates at around fifteen to twenty-five times per minute under normal conditions. When breathing is deepened and excitement increases, the pulses may go up to forty or fifty per minute, the aura expands, and the colour becomes brighter. These body states appear to be connected to the sympathetic-adrenal system.[12]

The experience of pleasure appears to be directly related to an ability to flow with our own natural rhythms. In painful states, we lack co-ordination with our own rhythms; in a pleasurable state our movements are smooth and rhythmic.[13]

The very definition of pleasure in Lowen's work is defined as '. . . the conscious perception of the rhythmic and pulsatory activity of the body'. The subject of biological rhythms, (biorhythms) has come under close scrutiny in recent years. The evidence is accumulating for a twenty three day physical cycle, a twenty eight day emotional cycle, and a thirty three day intellectual cycle.

Our internal rhythms appear to regulate our sleeping, waking, hunger, sexual arousal and moods, physical and mental alertness, and even, as noted with the effects on our blood, our vulnerability to drugs, poison and surgery.

The subject of biorhythms is taken very seriously in some quarters. Japan Air Lines, for example, refuses to let its pilots fly on 'down' days.

Dr Robert Moore of the University of California is convinced that the regulating mechanism of our internal body cycles is a tiny cluster of nerve cells, (the suprachiasmatic nucleus) located at the base of the brain. This is in the most primitive part of the brain, and is thus most linked to the rhythms of nature (as previously mentioned, these rhythms may be set by the low frequency waves generated by the Earth itself in its own magnetic and electric field).

Our biological clock-linked rhythms look as follows:

Midnight to 4 am   Most of your body functions are at their lowest ebb, but your hearing is at its sharpest (a fact not commonly appreciated by burglars); prehistoric man relied on this radar to protect him while he slept.

7 am   Your adrenal hormones peak, your heart rate increases, your body temperature rises and blood pulses more strongly through your body. Nature's own alarm.

8 am   Your sex-hormone production is at a peak (not at the traditional romantic hour of dusk).

9 am   You drink hot coffee without any discomfort. At this hour your body is least sensitive to pain. It may be your brain's peak time for production of its own opiates (enkephalins and endorphins); a time when pain-killing drugs are least needed. It was also a prime hour for the primitive hunter – a time when he was most likely to be injured by his quarry.

10 am   If you're introverted, your concentration and memory for acquiring new facts peak. Your efficiency is highest at this time.

Noon   Your body is most susceptible to the effects of alcohol. That's why a pub lunch can be disastrous to your performance for the rest of the day.

2 pm   Almost everyone experiences a post-lunch energy dip. It has less to do with what you've eaten than with your normal midday hormonal changes. This is the time when our savannah-dwelling ancestors laid down for a mid-day nap. The prime hunting times are morning and evening – most animals are dormant in the middle of the day.

3 pm   Extroverts are at their analytical and creative prime, and will be for several hours. Introverts are coming off their peak.

4 pm   Flushed? Perspiring? Breathing heavily? It's due to changes in your body metabolism as it gears up for the second half of the day.

5 pm   Your senses of smell and taste are most acute (a dangerous time for weight watchers). Your hearing has attained its second peak.

6 pm   Ironically, when most of us are sitting on commuter trains, buses or in our cars our potential for physical activity is at its peak. Strength and stamina have reached a daily high, though psychological factors can sap energy.

7 pm   Your temper and irritability can flare because of hormonal changes, your blood pressure peaks and emotions are shakiest.

8 pm   The day's food and water have been stored so the body's weight is at its maximum (not the time to step on the scales).

10 pm   Your hormone levels and body temperature are down; breathing slows; your body is at an overall performance low.

Midnight   Your body begins its hardest work, replacing dead cells and building new cells for the next day.[14]

This breakdown is not true for everyone of course. But using it as a guide, you might begin to notice your own daily rhythms, and thus plan your day accordingly where possible.

Taking note of your other, longer term rhythms can also be of benefit. I notice that I have a sleep pattern related to the moon phases – 2 weeks of sleep like death, followed by two weeks of erratic sleep. Likewise my overall daily energies are related – 2 weeks of high energy, two weeks of lethargy. I try to plan my work accordingly – writing during high energy times, and other, more routine and less mentally demanding work during my 'down' cycle.

True, not everyone lives a lifestyle where this is possible – but why not have a word with your employer, or spouse, and see if at least some adjustments in your routine are possible. Your increased productivity should soon be convincing.

Rhythmic routines are rooted in our biological past, and have contributed to our survival as a species. In *The Naked Ape*, Desmond Morris notes the pattern followed by humans in the establishment of their own natural routines:

1. You shall investigate the unfamiliar until it has become familiar;

2. you shall impose rhythmic repetition on the familiar;

3. you shall vary this repetition in as many ways as possible;

4. you shall select the most satisfying of these variations and develop these at the expense of others;

5. you shall combine and recombine these variations with one with another.[15]

He further points out that these rules apply to every spectrum of human activity at all ages, from a child in a sandpit to a composer writing a symphony.

Most of us realise that the dividing line between biology and psychology is so thin as to be almost non-existent, so although the next chapter looks specifically at the mind, we are increasingly aware that the mind and body are a single organism, and one is merely a reflection of the other.

Other societies have always known this; but the mind-oriented Western society has needed its own evolution to begin to accept this.

However, because we have so powerfully developed our minds, the door to our full body potential is also open. The implications of this, as we shall discover later, are staggering.

Chapter 5

THE COSMIC ROOTS OF THE MIND

> By the Law of Periodic Repetition, everything which
> has happened must happen again and again . . . the
> same Nature which delights in periodical repetition
> in the skies, is the Nature which orders the affairs of
> the Earth. Let us not underrate the value of that hint.
>
> MARK TWAIN

Growth. The most basic element that all things which live
on the Earth have in common. The alternative to growth is
stagnation and death.

When physical growth ceases, the organism shifts to
other types of growth; that of experience, of behaviour, or
of awareness. For mobile organisms, as awareness grows,
so does the surrounding world. For you and I, the
surrounding world is, if we allow ourselves to grow
enough, the Universe itself.

For humans, the path from physical growth, beginning
with a single cell, to the full flowering of our humanity, is
a long and seemingly convoluted process.

Finally, a pattern begins to emerge. We have long
known the developmental patterns of our physical bodies;
yet it is only through our more recent recognition (at least
in the Western world) that the mind and body are perfect
reflections of each other, that we can begin to see that all
levels of the human being follow similar patterns of
development. This is not to say that they develop simult-
aneously, nor that they necessarily develop fully.

Certain emotions may be frozen by one or several traumatic events at, say, the age of two. The physical body in
some aspect may be frozen at the same place. If this
opportunity for growth is not taken advantage of, that
person may never develop emotionally beyond the age of
two. Although the body will continue to *age*, it will not
develop. Next time you are around strangers, have a close

look at their faces and bodies – ask yourself: 'what age is he, or she really?' You will be surprised at how much you can read from the shape of the face and body, its posture, its general demeanour.

There are always opportunities for growth, chances to be taken. Life continually allows us to re-examine and re-evaluate ourselves, and gives us the tools to make our own changes.

Most of us have been aware of this process to a greater or lesser extent at certain times in our lives; perhaps not as something we could 'put our finger on', but rather as an uneasiness which tells us that we need to do *something*. These feelings, when seen clearly, are brightly lit neon signposts to our own personal fulfilment. Seeing them clearly is the problem.

When we realise that our own life is an integral part of all life, and follows the ebb and flow of the world around us, we can begin to look for and discover our own natural rhythms: to become increasingly masters of our own destiny, and to become fully *human*.

The following chapters deal principally with human psychology. Before approaching this in detail, it is important that we recognise the fact that a new view is emerging of what 'psychology' really means.

The traditional views of human psychology are now being replaced by a growing awareness that the human mind is the product not only of its training or education, but is also influenced by apparent external factors that are part of the natural environment. Some of these environmental factors affect the brain directly – and thus the functioning of the mind – and others, affect the body, with feedback to the mind, on both biochemical and emotional levels.

As we recognise that emotions are 'body events', and are only identified and categorised by the mind, then we begin to realise that anything which affects the body, from smog to the radiations of a television set, may produce biochemical feedback that the brain may identify as emotion.

The possibilities for confusion are boundless, and it's little wonder that we live in a society where the physical and psychological symptoms of 'overload' are endemic.

What is most disturbing to our sense of pleasure and well-being, is any upset to our own natural rhythms. Lowen states that:

> The feeling of pleasure that stems from a natural and undisturbed rhythm of life embraces all our activities and relationships. There is a time to work and a time to rest, a time to play and a time to be serious, a time to be together and a time to be alone. Too much togetherness can be as painful as too much aloneness, and too much play can be as dull as too much work. The rhythms that govern life are inherent in life; they cannot be imposed from without. Each individual knows what his rhythms are and knows by the feelings of pain or lack of pleasure when his rhythms are disturbed.[1]

As we have seen, there are many rhythms that are part of our own personal rhythms. Does this mean that we fulfill every rhythm all the time?

Yes and no. Our personal rhythms are like a river with many branches or tributaries, all blending in the mainstream of our life. Within the mainstream there may be whirlpools or eddies, backwaters and rapids; but all within the greater flow of the river.

Our lives move in a series of progressions, from one step to the next. To fulfill our Being, each step must be completed. We can still progress if a step is incomplete at a particular stage, but at a later time, we will be required to complete them, so that we can continue our progress through life.

At the physical level, we must complete each step – cell to embryo, embryo to foetus, foetus to infant, infant to adult. At the psychological level, each step must likewise be completed.

What then are the rhythms of our own development? The eminent French statistician Michel Gauquelin, in his book *Astrology and Science*, describes his surprising findings as he discovered a correlation between certain professions, and certain planetary positions.

His first discovery was that a high portion of eminent doctors were born with Mars or Saturn either rising or at the zenith (directly overhead). He found this true of doctors in every country he investigated, proving it to be no freak chance.

He further discovered that,

> when Mars appeared at the horizon or had just passed the highest point of its course across the sky, it was established that a greater number of people born at that time had a tendency to become great doctors, great athletes, or great soldiers. Future artists, painters or musicians, on the contrary, seemed to take care not to enter life at the times which suited doctors or athletes. Actors and politicians seemed to prefer to be born when Jupiter came to its rise and its zenith, whereas scientists chose an opposite time-table, seldom appearing at Jupiter's rise and zenith.[2]

Gauquelin is also quick to point out that he attaches absolutely no occult significance to this correlation; that in no way do planets 'cast a spell' on the unborn child, abruptly modifying the organism at birth.

> Why should it not happen the other way about: the child might have a predisposition to come into the world under certain cosmic conditions which corresponded to his biological constitution. In a way, the child would be waiting for the right time to be born, and this moment would merely be an indication of his biological makeup.[3]

Another interesting correlation was discovered between the position of certain planets at the time of birth of parents, and the positions of the same planets at the birth time of their children.

Gauquelin says:

> Planetary heredity followed rules of a consistency to satisfy the strictest critic. Its chief characteristic was its constancy, since it appeared in each of the areas studied, as much with the father as the mother, with the son as the daughter; and it regularly followed certain familiar genetic laws.[4]

Planets definitely connected to heredity in the study were Mars, Jupiter, Saturn, the Moon and Venus. There were more marked hereditary factors in children whose birth sky corresponded closely to their parents. The effect was constant in natural births, but disappeared when births were induced.[5]

The hereditary factor may well be what is behind the connection between certain professions and planetary positions. A child choosing to be born at a certain time would be choosing a time when his own constitution, already set by his genetics, is in alignment with whatever as yet unidentified Cosmic factors are in force.

There are other cycles and rhythms that are also part of our psychological development. Cosmic factors show a number of correlations with our ages at various critical times in our development. Gail Sheehy, in her remarkable books *Passages* and *Pathfinders*, identifies several critical turning points. These are discussed in detail later, but for the moment, let's look at the ages themselves:

18–22 years
23–27 years
28–33 years
34–45 years

If we lay out a comparison between these age groups, with the 11½ and 40 year sunspot cycles, Jupiter, Saturn (noted as especially significant by Gauquelin as birth planets) and the Saros cycle (mentioned in chapter 2), we get some interesting results:

Sheehy	Sunspots 11 yr	Sunspots 40 yr	Saros	Jupiter	Saturn
*(12–13)	11½			12	14 (½ cycle)
18–22	23		18½		
23–27				24	
28–33	34½				28½
34–45	46	40	37	36	42 (½ cycle)

* I have added this age group to the list as the onset of puberty, another major life passage.

This table is not intended to prove conclusively a connection between Cosmic events and human development, but there are some correlations that, to me at least, are highly suspicious. The preceding information falls loosely under the heading of astrology: Any natural cycle, in fact, related to astronomical movements could be called astrology.

Although I don't believe in astrology as a fortune telling device, there are certainly definite cycles that *do* relate to astronomy, as we have seen. So, I do not dismiss the idea that future *possibilities*, on a broad scale, may be forecast by analysing natural rhythms.

As a scientist, I am a professional sceptic. Yet there is too much evidence to dismiss, and I believe it is only now that we can begin to discover the true nature of Cosmic connections. Gauquelin has stated:

> After establishing the illusionary nature of the belief in astrological prediction, the scientist may still remain dissatisfied. After all, he knows that in the history of ideas, magic always precedes science, that the intuition of phenomena anticipates their objective knowledge. He feels intuitively, as men have always felt, that astrology may contain some truths . . .[6]

In *The Act of Creation*, Kroestler speaks of the 'Blocked Matrices' of science. A branch of science may become blocked for centuries, whereupon stagnation sets in. Often the blockage is psychological; it is waiting for the inner development of the scientists themselves:

> In the last few years, researchers have finally reopened the blocked matrices of astrology and replaced it with a new science. Science has supervised . . . mergers in the past by incorporating what used to be only superstition. In this century whole domains of the occult have been conquered by science, beginning with the 'key to the dreams'. Freud and Jung pioneered in this area, by reproaching science for having stopped at the thresholds of the illogical . . .
>
> The stage is set for the last act of the Cosmic drama, the most interesting and beautiful one. The rule of superstition ends here. A new science will replace the old Qabala of cosmic dreams; it will help us to access man's true place in the riddle of the Universe. We are indeed living through the turning point in human thought.[7]

I would like to give you my own definition of science,

from my book *The Cosmic Crystal Spiral*: *Science is the branch of mysticism that deals with the measurable.*

As our ability to measure the subtle influence of the Cosmos increases, less and less will become 'occult', and more and more will become 'science'. Does this mean that science is any less mysterious? Far from it. Indeed, the biggest argument in physics today is whether or not to use mystical terms to describe newly discovered behaviour of subatomic particles.

Beyond this, perhaps a talent we have lost in science, is the ability to see the mystery in everything. We are in a living miracle called Life. It is *all* mystical.

I had a dream a few years ago. I was a guru or some sort of spiritual teacher, whose teachings were being questioned; as proof of my teaching, a miracle was demanded of me. I put out the word that those who wanted to see a miracle should assemble in a particular field early one morning. That morning I stepped up onto a dais, and said to the multitude, 'You wanted to see a miracle – look behind you;' and walked away.

It was the sunrise.

Chapter 6

PSYCHOLOGICAL RHYTHMS

The attainment of autonomy is manifested by the
release or recovery of three capacities: awareness,
spontaneity and intimacy.

ERIC BERNE, MD
The Games People Play (1964)

We know that in the development of our minds and in our
learning through experience of the world around us, that
we all follow a parallel set of patterns. Not that our
patterns are identical, but everyone progresses in a series
of steps or stages, regardless of what we are learning;
whether it is how to use a spoon, higher mathematics, to
hover a helicopter, or to develop our emotions and our
capacity for intimacy.

First comes a burst of initial learning; then a plateau,
and usually a slight slide backwards; then another burst of
learning as the previous stage is integrated and new connections are made. This is the tug-of-war between our
neophilic and neophobic urges. The former drives us on to
new exploration and new experience. The latter demands
we take refuge in the safe and familiar. In a healthy
human there is always a pull back and forth between
them; becoming unbalanced towards neophobia brings
stagnation, whereas unbalance in neophilia is a headlong
rush to disaster. The whole pattern of expansion and contraction in human development and culture is rooted in
these two urges. The purpose? To push us on to new
learning but to make it as safe as possible.

Recent studies of the brain have uncovered the mechanism of learning, which concerns not so much the brain
cells themselves, but rather the myriad of connections
between the cells. A memory is a pattern of connections
between certain cells that become biochemically strengthened. New learning strengthens new connections and the

cells involved then fire into a new pattern. Thus even the function of the brain is rhythmic – each thought or memory is a particular rhythm of brain cell activity.

In diagrammatic form, learning looks like this:

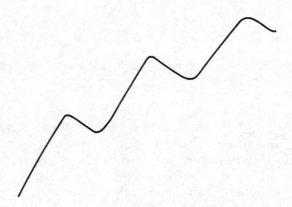

It is the classic 'three steps forward and slide one back' pattern, and we all do it. At each plateau, we feel stuck, or a failure, or wonder if we are back where we started.

This is also an expansion and contraction pattern. We expand outwards through the accumulation of new information and experiences and then we then contract inwards to integrate those experiences (that is, to strengthen the intercellular connections). Then, starting from who we have become at that point of integration, we again expand outwards to receive new inputs, and to redefine ourselves yet again.

These expansion and contraction patterns occur at a number of stages and levels of our development:

1. The ultimate expansion, life; the ultimate contraction, death. However, this may be viewed in exactly the *opposite* way: life is a contraction into the limitations of the physical body; death is an expansion back into the larger realm of the Cosmos.

2. The long cycle expansions and contractions lasting

many years in our psychological and emotional development.

3. Seasonal cycles in body rhythms.

4. Cycles of relationships, lasting from days to minutes.

5. Daily cycles regulated by sleep, and so forth.

6. Short term, emotional cycles lasting minutes or seconds

As suggested throughout this book, these rhythms all correspond in some way to outer rhythms, although the dividing line between 'inner' and 'outer' is very fine indeed. Our very sense of well-being is almost certainly related to whether or not we flow with our own natural rhythms relating to the world around us. There is a time to expand, a time to contract. If we try to force ourselves to adopt a rhythm that is not our own, we become distressed or bored, and depression can set in.

When we are younger, expansion or contraction tends to take on a more physical aspect: we test ourselves in sport, adventure, sex. Our physical being has its own bounds to explore. Even in childhood our physical body follows the same type of developmental pattern: spurts of growth, followed by plateaus of integration – the classic awkwardness of the budding teenager as he or she integrates physical, mental and emotional growth.

As we grow older and we become confident of our physical being, we begin to develop our mental and emotional lives further, where, once again, the same 'stair-step' pattern appears. The possibilities for growth in these areas of our personality go far beyond the physical opportunities, and concurrently, the spiritual dimension begins to open and develop.

In any lifetime, any or all of these dimensions can grow to a certain degree, but inevitably they are interconnected. A personality which is over-developed in one area or another, cries out for rebalance. It is this tension that is a prime opportunity for growth – or self-destruction.

Gail Sheehy, in her brilliant books *Passages* and *Path-finders*, has identified a number of distant stages of human development. At each stage a crisis appears – a demand for integration and re-assessment. Out of each one emerges a new sense of self, a new sense of values, and a renewed sense of purpose. These are the opportunities – if they are grasped.

The other option is to avoid making any changes, or to go only part of the way. However, changes not made at one stage, have a way of re-appearing at the next; except that the next time, they are harder, and require more energy to accomplish.

In my own work as a counsellor, I have found Ms Sheehy's stages to be exceedingly accurate. The same is true of participants in my seminars where I have talked about life cycles. As her work was focussed on adult life, I have added the earlier age-groups, from conception through to teenage. For the material on pre-adult cycles, I draw on my work as a counsellor, my personal memories and experiences, the responses of many people in seminars and workshops, as well as the written source material listed at the end of the book.

In the material on conception through to early childhood, the question of reincarnation may arise in some readers' minds. Ultimately, it is not important whether certain life patterns arise from previous lives, or spontaneously. The life currently being lived is the only one of any significance, and if reincarnation is a fact, whatever lessons necessary for this lifetime are brought forward to be dealt with in the *here and now*. As you grow and progress through your own life, you may well discover, as I did, that each stage of personal growth and development in this lifetime *feels* like a past life. Since I was born, I feel as if I have lived at least half a dozen lives. The opening of the personality to reveal the true Self, is a process of unfoldment – of one petal opening after another, ultimately to reveal the *real you* in the centre.

As I shed each layer of my personality that is no longer useful to me, what emerges is a new sense of self, with an inner feeling of solidarity, of reality. Each layer that is shed turns out to have been an illusion, and might be labelled 'who I am not'. It might look like this:

Or, it is often drawn like this:

The thousand petal lotus – with the jewel in the centre. The jewel is the real you, the petals are really experiences and beliefs of 'who you are not' – that is, illusions. As each petal falls away, the other petals become clearer, or perhaps seen for the first time. It is a process of progressively peeling away layers of beliefs that no longer serve us.

Each cycle brings up our ideas and beliefs for re-examination, so that we may discard or renew them. Then follows a period of re-integration, a time to try out the 'new us'. It is the 'stair-step' pattern from the beginning of the chapter:

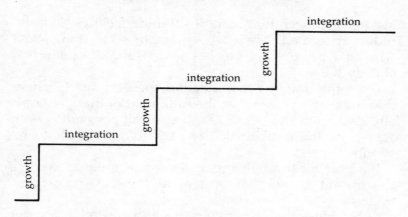

This is also an expansion-contraction cycle:

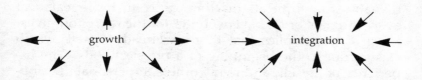

Here are the various stages of growth and unfoldment, especially the pressure points, the points of identity crisis:

CONCEPTION
PRE-BIRTH
BIRTH
BIRTH – 2 YEARS
2 YEARS – 18 YEARS

18–22 YEARS
23–27 YEARS
28–33 YEARS
34–45 YEARS/THE MIDLIFE STAGE
BEYOND MIDLIFE

Conception

Conception is a separate and distinct stage, for in the

instant of conception, many of the life feelings and attitudes are formed. Also at this moment, everything about who that person will be, is known – the life pattern is already there.

Does this imply predestination, or destiny? I believe that the pattern is set, but the fulfilment of that pattern is always a matter of choice. The inner call goes out at each stage, but the individual may or may not choose to respond.

It is possible through age-regression techniques to relive the instant of our conception, and discover our own patterns.

Other ideas that are involved with conception are our attitudes to love and sex. Did we experience our conception as an act of love, as an act of lust, or even anger or attack? Subtle beliefs about the opposite sex and our own sexuality can form at this time, only to be repeated at every intimate or sexual encounter for the rest of our lives.

All of this implies that there is already a 'self' which exists prior to the beginning of a physical body. The experience of myself, and many others in personal development courses and groups bears this out. Those who have relationships with their parents suitable for discussing this matter have found that their memories of their conception are accurate. The relationship with the parents is also established to a degree in this moment; was I wanted or not? was I conceived in love?

The feelings and attitudes established in this first instant arise, in one form or another, at all of the regular, cyclic crisis points, as you attempt to return to that same state of beingness that existed before your body began – who you were at the moment when your body began its own Cosmic explosion; your own 'Big Bang', as your body exploded into Life.

Pre-birth

The time from conception to our emergence into the outer world is a time of major psychological growth. There is a growing body of research suggesting that much of our underlying psychological development takes place in the womb. Our basic feelings of how the world is going to be, are transmitted to us through our mother.

Recent research has also shown that our basic life rhythms are established here, such as our sleeping patterns; late-to-bed mothers bore late-to-bed babies, and early-rising mothers bore early-rising babies. Months before birth, the mother and baby are beginning to synchronise their rhythms to each other.

One of the most basic rhythms sets itself to the mother's heartbeat. The 72 beats-per-minute rhythm has an enormously calming effect when we are feeling disturbed – soothing music is often paced at or near this rhythm. We rock back and forth at this rhythm to comfort ourselves when in a state of stress. The next time you see someone speaking in public, notice whether they are rocking back and forth, and time it against your own heartbeat.

There is evidently a sophisticated communication system between mother and unborn child – the child sends signals to the mother, and responds to her response to them. This takes place on a level that is often unnoticed by the mother. Thomas Verney, in *The Secret Life of the Unborn Child*, states:

> The newborn's response to his mother's hugs, stroking, looks and other cues is based on his long acquaintance with her prior to birth.[1]

> What happens after birth is an elaboration of, and depends on, what happened prior to it.[2]

The child in the womb is also part of his mother's emotional system. Chemical messages pass freely through the placenta, so the child is totally aware of his mother's emotional state – although he is unaware that there is anything other than himself at this stage. So his mother's emotions become his, although they are events that happen to him, rather than are felt by him.

Unborn children are very resilient, and the normal daily upsets are not harmful. However, a major traumatic event happening to the mother can and does have a major impact on the child.

Likewise, if the mother is emotionally ill, the child may well develop the same patterns of emotional illness.

Mothers with major psychiatric illness such as schizo-phrenia often produce children who themselves have a high rate of emotional and physical problems.

None of this is meant to imply that all emotions experi-enced from the mother are harmful – quite the contrary. The normal daily emotional fluctuations of the mother are in fact quite useful to begin conditioning the child's own emotional system. Thus, the mother's patterns, in this case the emotions, begin to imprint on the child.

Birth

It is astonishing how many of our basic attitudes about life are established in the delivery and first few minutes after birth. Often, of course, these are just reinforcements of the womb experiences. Most of our basic life patterns are set between the time of conception and the first ten minutes of our lives. These will be reinforced and compounded time and time again, until the later life crises begin to bring them up to be dealt with.

Why are they established in the first place?

We live in a world of polarity. The black words on this page stand out because of the whiteness of the page. A thing is often seen the most clearly in contrast with its opposite. Night is noticed as an absence of day, pleasure by the contrast to pain, and so on.

We tend to establish in our life patterns, beliefs and ideas that are opposite to our real nature, to who we really are.

These bottom line beliefs are the most powerful, as they tend to run our lives until identified, and their opposite (who we really are) is noticed.

The beliefs that arise from birth establish our basic world-view, and our view of ourselves. The Loving Relationship Training calls them 'Personal Laws'.

A personal law is your most negative belief about your-self. It is a bottom line belief that all other beliefs stem from. My own personal law was that God hates/hurts me. This was for abandoning Him, for separating myself from Him and taking on a body.

Incidentally, everyone on the Earth has this belief, but

manifested in a personal law it can take a number of different forms.

The feelings of this developed for me in the last few months in the womb – a feeling of being trapped and in pain. Then a difficult delivery, with my mother in a great deal of pain (belief: I am a bad person because I cause women pain). My mother was given ether, which passed to me through the placenta – I thought I was being killed for hurting her (beliefs: women kill me; if I 'push hard' in life, I'll be killed). I was then pulled out with forceps (belief: I'm a failure, I can't even get myself born). I was then placed on a cold surface, while the doctors worked on my mother (beliefs: the world is a cold and noisy place; I am ignored when I need help the most), and wasn't allowed to go to the breast (belief: I can't get my needs met). I was then wheeled away to the nursery without any contact with my mother (belief: women abandon me).

All of this in the first ten minutes. My birth certificate reads – Type of Birth: *Normal*.

It is this way, for several generations of Western children. Is it any wonder that we view the world as we do? Heartless, noisy, dangerous and unsupportive.

Dr Verney says:

> Everything we have learned in the past decade tells us we could not have devised a worse way of birth if we tried. Yet many children in the western world continue to be born in a setting that might be appropriate for a computer, but that is wildly inappropriate for a human being.[3]

We all know about first impressions, and how powerful they can be, as they are really an 'outgrowth' of the part of us that defends and protects us. They are a vital part of our survival mechanism – the ability to size up a situation quickly for its possible threat.

However, this mechanism may well work against us psychologically at birth. Our psychology was *not* designed for modern birth methods, as we have seen. Even in the best possible situation – a loving and caring mother and father, a loving and caring doctor or midwife, and soothing birth conditions, there is still bound to be trauma.

The child in a loving womb is at peace with himself and

his universe, of which, by the ninth month he is profoundly aware. There are minor upsets of course, but they are not lasting and may be quite helpful.

Birth is a prolonged and profound physical shock. There is pain as the child is thrust into the birth canal and contractions progress, often for hours, although there are also moments of intense pleasure as skin to skin contact is made for the first time.

To a child sensitised to the perfect world of the womb, the new flood of sensations can be overwhelming – and this is in the best circumstances . . .

Fortunately, techniques such as re-birthing are now available to help us sort out our traumas, and harvest the learning they hold for us.

In the processes of sorting ourselves out, we know that when we get to survival issues arising around the time of birth, we are getting near to the bottom line, because all of our underlying unresolved issues originated out of a feeling of threat-to-survival.

We know that there is a sensory mechanism that takes over when the nervous system goes into overload. Many quarters of medical science now acknowledge this, and it shows that nothing goes unrecorded, even when the body is 'frozen'. It is this mechanism that we tap into when we begin to unwind the traumas that have kept us 'stuck'.

For me, the basic patterns or beliefs of my life, all lead to the same conclusion: If you want to live in a body, *God is gonna get you!*

So, I better punish myself before God does, because He'll do a lot better job of it than I will!

A lot of us have this pattern!

My life lesson has been to work through those beliefs, and to discover that their *opposite* has been true.

In working through those lies, to finally see the biggest lie of all: that God hates/hurts me for having a body. In one of the most powerful moments of my life, during a re-birthing session, I suddenly saw that just the opposite was true: that God loves and cares for me, and that sometime in a distant past in taking on a body, *I* had lost my feeling of connection with *HIM*, and thought *He* had abandoned *me*.

And that all the times in my life I had felt abandoned

were in fact unconsciously bringing up that feeling for me to work through, and therein healing me in the most profound way: helping me to return to my own Source.

Through consciously knowing how the process works, you can heal yourself by taking full advantage of the feelings that arise. You have probably had utterly disastrous relationships, as I have – but you can grow in spite of them by working with yourself, healing yourself. As have I. These relationships are there to show you what your beliefs are that don't serve you.

Then one day you will meet someone who is conscious of the patterns, and is also willing to work through their issues hand in hand with you. The person to whom this book is dedicated is such a person to me. Even in our worst moments we are conscious of the healing that is taking place, moving us both a step closer towards our Source.

Birth–2 years

The identity crisis that characterises this cycle of life is precisely that one *has* an identity, a separate identity; that one is an individual, and is a separate being from mother.

It is in this experience that we recreate our own 'separate-from-God' experience. In most animals this separate self-identity develops with weaning. Where weaning doesn't occur at a natural time, a debilitating dependency develops in the young animal, which frequently results in premature death, should it reach adulthood.

In humans, such a personality is called a 'mamma's boy', with all of its connotations of dependency. Such a dependency can become transferred to a mate, and is one of the major life patterns that comes up for most people at each crisis period.

Most humans have this pattern to some degree, and true adulthood never occurs without resolving it. If not resolved sooner, this is one pattern that comes up most forcefully at midlife.

THE PULSE OF LIFE

2 years–18 years

Although a few patterns are developed during this time, it is mostly a period of reinforcing patterns that have already been developed. The human is very resilient, and although a single traumatic event *may* 'freeze' a person at a particular age, it usually takes more than one event.

Why do we keep repeating events until they freeze us emotionally?

Life is about learning, and the things which we come into life to learn about, are those things that we created through our infant traumas.

It is important to recognise that *we choose our traumas*. Pre-conception memories of thousands of people have confirmed what many beliefs have taught for a very long time – we *choose* our parents. Not only that, we choose a set of parents who will give us the environment of womb, birth, childhood and so on, to give us the learning that we need. In other words, the parents who will create the proper traumas for us.

The Earth is a planet of learning through and about emotions. Our physical bodies are capable of intense emotions and it is through them that the most profound learning can take place.

At the two year old stage, the real crisis for both parent and child is the development of language in the child. Up to this time, the cerebral cortex, has been growing and expanding its capacity for storage and reason. By the age of two, the average child has a vocabulary of around 300 words; by the age of four, this figure has tripled.

The crisis for the parents arises when the child can begin to say what it wants, what it likes, and what it *doesn't* want or like!

Up to this point it is not uncommon for many parents, especially with the first child, to relate to the infant almost as they would a pet. Something to be cuddled and cared for, something to be loved and played with, but without a mind of its own.

Then the 'Terrible Two's' hit. The child not only has a mind of its own, but it frequently and vocally demonstrates this!

It is not unusual for the parent-child relationship to shift

58

dramatically at this time, and if the mother tends to with-
draw from the child (even in self-preservation!), the child
may well experience abandonment. Yet this is usually a
repetition and a reinforcement of the original birth trauma –
the removal from the mother at birth.

With the development of language comes an increased
ability to evaluate. Now, the words and actions of the
parents, and later friends and society generally, begin to
give a mixed message: our words often do not agree with
our actions. What a child senses and what a child is told
are often opposite. The opportunities for reinforcement of
earlier patterns are boundless.

By the time we are into teenage, our patterns are well
set. As we begin to take on the mantle of adulthood, we
begin to work through these patterns. We learn as we go,
and throw up all the incompleted lessons in a series of
crises that recur at intervals for the rest of our adult lives.

18–22 years

This is the first of Gail Sheehy's adult developmental
crises, which she calls 'Pulling-up-Roots'. I see this as a
rapid series of expansions and contractions, of flapping
our wings furiously in the world, to fall exhausted back
into the nest for a while to recuperate. The nest may be
our parents' home, or a group of our contemporaries. One
phrase in *Passages* stood out for me about this period: 'The
Battle to Invent Ourselves'.

The prime characteristic of this whole crisis phase is the
establishment of our own sense of individuality. We begin
breaking the bonds with our parents – or at least stretch-
ing them – to confront the unknown and take chances,
although usually with the safety of our family home or
familiar surroundings or institutions to fall back on.

Very few develop true individuality at this stage. We
mostly substitute one set of parents for another – a mate,
an authoritarian social or spiritual group, or a group of
contemporaries. In my time of uprooting, the hippies were
the rebels, the 'individuals'. Today it is the punks. Strange,
but somehow they all look alike!

This is a time of extreme vulnerability for the young

fledgling human. There are plenty of vultures about with promises of a new identity, a new destiny, an open hand full of ultimate truth, 'if only you will follow me . . .'

Above all during this period, is the underlying fear 'that we are still really kids who can't take care of ourselves'.

23 years–27 years

The next cycle, the 'Trying Twenties', sees us finally establishing a provisional identity to:

> . . . shape a Dream, that vision of ourselves which will generate energy, aliveness, and hope. To prepare for a lifework. To find a mentor if possible. And to form the capacity for intimacy, without losing in the process whatever consistency of self we have thus far mustered.[4]

We create powerful illusions of ourselves at this period – and we often get locked into 'shoulds'. We *should* find a career, a mate, conform, or not conform . . . These visions carry us through, and inspite of their illusion of permanence, they will be among the first things that we will shed in our later climb to the true Self.

This is a time for building our strengths, not assessing our weaknesses, but as we approach our 30's, our surety begins to crumble. The suppressed parts of us we have ignored begin to surface, and if given a chance to do so, will continue to surface into our 40's.

The late 20's are a time of jolting us from our comfortable and safe view of ourselves and of the world – when a new reality begins to emerge.

The astrologers will tell us that Saturn, the planet of Learning, has returned to the place it was in the sky at the time of our birth. Of the 20's Sheehy says:

> . . . a fantastic mystery story waits to be written . . . It races with excitement and jeopardy, fools us with false villains, diverts us from the real villains that are the divisions within ourselves . . . , and leads us down secret passageways in search of our missing personality parts.[5]

PSYCHOLOGICAL RHYTHMS

28–33 years

The transition to the 30's largely involves tearing down most of what we have built up in the 20's, and putting it back together again within a new vision of who we are.

Old issues and patterns re-emerge at this time, challenging us to re-assess and re-evaluate ourselves. Parental influences begin to fade a bit, and we begin to take more responsibility for our own vision of ourselves. The difference between who we really are, and who our parents taught us we are, begins to emerge.

Marriages take a real pounding around this time, as we begin the process of re-evaluation, and divorces are common in this phase. However, where marriages endure, there is almost always a new set of agreements to accommodate 'who we are becoming'.

None of this is likely to go smoothly; nor is it *meant* to. There are plenty of hurdles and challenges. Growth is, by its nature, a painful process, and the transition to the 30's is the opening of the doorway to midlife – the time when we have an opportunity to discover our true Selves, and become Real.

34–45 years – the midlife stage

The most startling thing I have noticed about people coming into their 'midlife crisis', is that anything undigested or incomplete from the first half of their life, literally from conception onward, forcefully blasts its way to the surface. It is not surprising that many people have a 'second childhood' around this time, as early unresolved issues surface.

It is a time when a man's feminine traits begin to emerge and strengthen; a time when a woman's masculine traits are called forth. It is a time of tidying up, a time of completion, a time to finish the unfinished task of self-discovery, and then to get on with being who you really are.

It is, needless to say, a daunting task for most. Gail Sheehy describes it as: 'seeing the dark first, disassembling ourselves, then glimpsing the light, and gathering our parts into a renewal.'[6]

Many researchers now agree that the transition to mid-life may be as difficult as adolescence. Sheehy says: 'What is disassembling is that narrow self we have thus far put together in a form tailored to please the culture and other people.'[7]

This is a time of mourning and depression also. Mourning for lost illusions; depression that is a letting go process. Before this time, we are almost all caught up in taking our identity from society, an outworking of our parental conditioning. Midlife, should we allow ourselves a full-blown crisis, becomes a time of learning to act on our own *inner* authority. Before, the carry-over from our parents was that if we were 'good' boys and girls and did what our parents (or society) wanted us to do, we would be liked and rewarded. It is an illusion.

Many of us, of course, are happy enough with our illusions, and are unwilling to face the pain of change. Unfortunately issues not dealt with at midlife will keep popping up again in the 50's and 60's, or even later. Many people who are stuck and unwilling to make changes begin to die at around this time. What is the purpose of keeping going in a lifetime where there is no further learning?

Gail Sheehy states: 'The most important words in mid-life are – Let go. Let it happen to you. Let it happen to your partner. Let the feelings. Let the changes.'[8]

If you are willing to do this, you will emerge from this period with a strengthened sense of self, an inner knowing of who you *really* are, and with a renewed sense of purpose, a sense of energy and direction in your life to fulfill your own purpose in being.

I am personally comforted, and not at all surprised, that Muhammad received his enlightenment at the age of 40.

Beyond Midlife

The stages beyond midlife are important, of course, but their patterns are largely set by the handling of the midlife period. Should the pressures of change be ignored, they will just keep repeating, but with greater intensity each time. The Inner Being will not let you rest.

PSYCHOLOGICAL RHYTHMS

If you allow yourself the changes, experience the pain of growth, the depression of dying illusions, then the full flowering of your human potential is assured. And who can say what course that may take?

Here is a summary of the adult stages:

18–22
1. Establish our separate individuality

23–27
1. Establishing a provisional identity

2. Cultivate a capacity for intimacy

3. Prove our own uniqueness

28–33
1. Re-appraise our relations

2. Re-assess career and family

3. Re-order or intensify commitments

38–45
1. Mortality becomes real

2. Examine gaps between personal illusions and realities

*3. A strengthened sense of self

*4. A renewed sense of purpose

---

* These are the prizes for a successful 'passage'. You are well on your way to becoming Human.

Chapter 7

THE RHYTHM OF RELATIONSHIPS

The antidote to loneliness is not togetherness; it is intimacy.

RICHARD BACH
The Bridge Across Forever (1984)

Although we are looking at human relationships here, it should be realised that the other kingdoms experience relationships also.

We have seen those of the mineral kingdom that create stars, galaxies, planets; and, the relationships between the parts of our own planet that give it Life at the mineral level of being.

Relationships in the mineral kingdom are cyclic over very long time periods. In the plant kingdom, the relationships become more complex, and the basic rhythms of the kingdom are seasonal. Other relationships relate to climate, rainfall patterns, and other plants and animals living in the same environment.

We know now that certain trees exchange information chemically, and that plants are sensitive to the psychic emanation of humans. How many more relationships will be discovered? I suspect we have barely scratched the surface.

The animal kingdom sees the development of relationships at a more personal level than plants. At one end of the scale, there is the loose relationships of microscopic animal life, which are still rather plant-like in the relationship sense. At the other end of the scale are the larger, more complex animals with relationships similar to our own – families, mates, caring, and nurturing.

As mentioned in chapter 1, the Universe is moving into greater complexity, and therefore, so is Life on the Earth.

THE RHYTHM OF RELATIONSHIPS

With increased biological complexity comes an increased capacity for relationships.

Our own human relationships go through a number of natural cycles and rhythms.

The first rhythm, as with the Universe itself, is expansion and contraction.

One of the most important thoughts that is underlined in Sondra Ray's book, *Loving Relationships* is that 'love brings up anything unlike itself'. The purpose is for healing. Love is the natural state of being – all of the other feelings, although a natural part of the learning process of human life, are feelings which tend to get in the way of love. Love is the state of connection with the Source, and therefore anything that is not love keeps you from the source of your own 'beingness'.

Relationships of all kinds exist to help you get back to your Source, so relationships are designed to bring up all of the things that keep you from that Source.

Have you ever noticed how your personal relationships go through times of closeness, followed by times of 'apartness'? And aren't these 'apartness' times usually associated with some feeling of hurt, or resentment, or anger?

If so, this is the natural order of things, and it means that you have a good relationship. Does that sound as if it is the wrong way round? Do you believe that good relationships should be cosy and stable and that it is desirable for them always to be like that?

Remember, growth is life. Stagnation, lack of growth is death. Unless you and your partner are growing, you are dead and so is your relationship. Growth always has periods of discomfort and uncertainty. If love brings up that which is unlike itself for healing, then a loving relationship *must* bring up anger and hurt and trauma.

Expansion and contraction are part of the healing process of relationships as shown in the diagram overleaf.

Between any two people, there is a body of unresolved inner issues, the issues you have chosen subconsciously to bring up in your relationship for healing. It is the nature of attraction that two people will be drawn together who have unresolved issues that interlock; that is, your issues will be part of your partner's and vice versa.

In the coming together process, the usual pattern is to

THE PULSE OF LIFE

EXPANDED

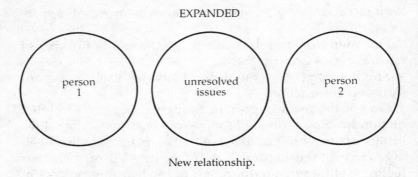

New relationship.

CONTRACTED

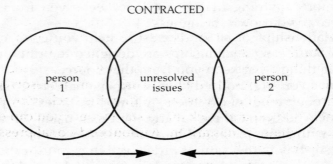

Bonds form drawing partners together.

EXPANDED

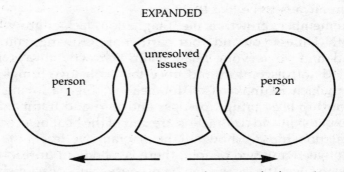

Bonds are stretched as each partner resolves issues that have arisen.
Then the whole cycle repeats itself.

avoid these issues in the beginning of the relationship,
and to develop bonds of attachment that are strong enough
to endure when the *real* issues of the relationship begin to

come up at a later time – usually three to six months after the conception of a new relationship. If these bonds have not developed in this time, the relationship usually breaks up at the three to six month period, when the real issues arise. Have you noticed this pattern in your own relationships?

So, as the relationship draws the partners closer together, eventually the deeper, unresolved issues begin to surface, usually those issues from the time of conception to birth of each partner.

This is the point where we wonder what has gone wrong. As we contract and get closer to our partner, suddenly anger, resentment, hatred and other unpleasant feelings surface.

The answer is that nothing has gone wrong. In fact, it is going very right. You have become close enough for it to be 'safe' for these issues to surface and be worked through.

When the emerging issues become too intense, and fear begins to set in (which is why the issues are unresolved in the first place), there is usually a drawing back from your partner. You expand back into a state where you can each work on whatever has arisen, without additional pressure from the relationship.

You are often unaware of what is happening, and this is usually a time when you have your first quarrel, and don't speak or see each other for a few days. Then, as whatever has arisen begins to dissipate, you once again feel the love; the relationship begins to draw closer again, and all is rosy – until the next time!

If you are able to recognise this pattern as it occurs, you can use your relationship constructively to further your own growth as well as your partner's.

Firstly, stay together and work at your issues. Secondly, allow yourself a healing time together after you have dealt with your issues. Lots of love-making, lots of talk, lots of sharing of experiences. Communication is of the absolute essence.

Remember that you are in a relationship for healing, and your partner is trying to heal you, even when he or she is screaming at you!

You will probably notice in your own relationships that there is another personal pattern related to expansion and contraction. When a powerful issue arises, do you tend to draw into yourself and cut off communication – *contract*, or do you tend to push your partner even harder – *expand*?

If you are an expander, you will say things like: 'Will you *listen* to me,' or 'Come back here!'

If you are a contracter, your bywords are: 'Leave me alone' or 'Go away'.

Expanders almost always attract contracters, and vice versa. Does this mean that if he or she always contracts and you always expand, that ultimately communication is impossible? No, but it does mean that you have to work hard on yourself – an expander needs to learn to stop, to slow down their headlong rush, and a contracter needs to learn not to draw into themselves quite so much. This is a basic challenge of almost every relationship.

The expansion-contraction cycle is by no means limited to difficult or unpleasant situations, although through our pre-birth and birth experiences our bodies can become so conditioned to pain that we actually identify our 'aliveness' by the amount of pain we feel. In a contraction situation where we are extremely close to someone, the pleasure may become so threatening that we need to back off. We can actually have to develop a *tolerance* for pleasure.

Relationships also follow the stair-step pattern, which looks a bit like this:

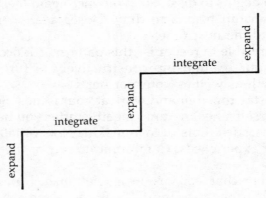

In the expansion stage of a relationship, we begin to learn about our new partner – their likes and dislikes, something about who they are. This stage is laden with illusions, with us acting out the parts we think our new partner wants, and projecting onto our partner the image of the person we *want* them to be.

In the contraction or integration stage, the realities begin to creep in, and we re-evaluate the relationship based on who we now perceive our partner to be. This is also the time for a healthy re-evaluation of ourselves; if nothing else, to see how we got ourselves into this new mess!

Eventually, we will reach an integration stage where a new realisation dawns:

This pattern is just like the last one!

And so, to some degree, will every one be, because the patterns of your partner are just a reflection of your own patterns. You can only attract a partner who is just like you. One of the basic laws of the Universe is that *like attracts like*. In this instance, the 'alikeness' is a mutual need of each partner, whether they be an expander or a contracter, to move towards the centre of their respective cycles.

If we are using expansion and contraction to its fullest, we *can* change ourselves, because our own personal lives go through expansion and contraction cycles as well. This is our relationship with *ourselves* (or our Selves!) Because the world reflects ourselves back to us, every response we see in the world around us is somehow a projection of who we really are.

In an expansion cycle we are actively out in the world, busy, gathering new experiences. In contraction, we look inward to discover what the sum total of those experiences is, to get a clearer picture of ourselves.

I have found the following diagram useful:

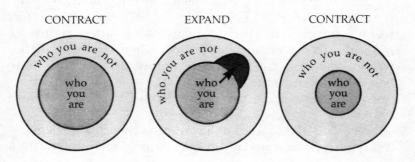

69

In my own expansion periods, I often discover things by trying something new. Every time I do this, I gain a clearer idea of who I am and who I am not. Life for me has been a process of elimination, of trial and error. Many of you will have had a clear idea of direction almost from the beginning. Others, like myself, need to be seekers. It is all part of the natural order of things.

The 'who you are not' circle also applies to relationships. Each new relationship is a reflection of you. If the reflections do not match on enough levels, or the relationship completes its purpose by you growing through the issues of the relationship, then it will break up. It has served its purpose.

For some people, one relationship over an extended period can provide all the necessary growth opportunities. For others, many relationships may be necessary. Either is fine. Again, it is in the nature of things.

Although the relationship is the primary stimulus to growth, it would be a mistake to assume that both parties grow at the same rate, or that the issues that arise will be mutual. Each individual has his or her own rhythms and cycles. The Law of Synchronicity which says that when something is right, all events synchronise around it, will assure that you attract a partner who will provide you (and themselves) with good growth opportunities. Often partners will 'take turns' growing; one partner will provide a stable base for the other's growth period, and vice versa.

Sheehy points out numerous studies of marriage, which show happiness at its peak in the first year. By the second year, satisfaction begins to drop, reaching rock bottom in the seventh year when divorces are the most likely to occur.[1]

Another pattern which appears in relationships is the pattern of your own early development. Do you often start feeling trapped in a new relationship after about six months? This is around the time when 'trapped in the womb' feelings start for many unborn infants. This time between six and nine months is a time when many of us need to 'escape' from the entrapment of a serious relationship.

Were you abandoned at 18 months by a parent leaving or dying? Then 18 months into a new relationship is a danger point for you, when you may subconsciously create the situation of being 'abandoned' by your partner.

By understanding our own early development, we can anticipate such pressure points in our relationships, and be aware that the feelings arising at these points are old feelings resurfacing, and are not being created by the partner.

A wonderful line from the *Course in Miracles* (Arkana) is: 'You are never upset for the reason you think you are.' As I am able to remember this more and more in my own relationships, to remember that what is happening inside me is almost always an old pattern resurfacing, I am more able to deal with those feelings in other ways besides taking them out on my partner.

By my awareness of my own 'danger points', and my partner's we are now able to use our relationship consciously to identify and work through old patterns as they emerge. My partner and I are, ultimately, each other's therapists, as indeed are all partners in all relationships.

The aspect of our personality that grows through this expansion and contraction cycle is our capacity for intimacy. The most powerful drive to develop real intimacy in our relationships comes from our sense of aloneness. Richard Bach has said: 'The antidote to loneliness is not togetherness, it is intimacy.'

Intimacy is a state of knowing someone else as well as you know yourself; and from that knowing, reaching the point of acceptance. The key words here are 'knowing' and 'acceptance'.

The state of higher beingness, which we call enlightenment or Christhood, is truly a state of pure self-acceptance. It cannot be reached without intimate self-knowledge. Because self-knowledge comes from self-reflection, intimate knowledge of someone else is a powerful self-mirror.

One of the most difficult aspects of self-knowledge is accepting the parts of ourselves we don't want to face – our own 'dark side'.

In a recent series of films, the hero had to come into contact with, and overcome the dark side of the 'Force', represented by an evil villain who had turned from his own light side to his own darkness. At one point, the hero discovered that the villain was potentially himself, if he allowed his own dark nature to manifest.

At midlife, especially, we are thrown up against our own shadow self. Our deeply suppressed or ignored parts resurface to haunt us. Because love brings up anything unlike itself, our relationships at this part of our natural cycle become especially important, as the things that *are* the dark side, are the things that are unlike love.

In addition, as a result of the midlife stage being a time of becoming Real, all of our 'unrealness' will re-emerge. As we being to realise the ultimate power of Love, the power to strip away all illusions about the Self, we see that it is truly the power for our own Christhood to emerge.

In attracting our partners, a certain set of patterns emerges. Because our own patterns are connected to our parents, and have set up our personalities for our particular learning situation, these patterns are mostly parent-centred. One thing of which you can be absolutely certain is that anything that is unresolved with your parents, will come up in your relationships!

These patterns are listed below, and are from Sondra Ray's book *Loving Relationships*.

> **Pattern 1** – you tend to attract partners who re-create your parents' *personalities*
>
> **Pattern 2** – you tend to re-create the kind of *relationships* you had with your parents
>
> **Pattern 3** – you tend to re-create the kind of relationships your parents had *with each other*
>
> **Pattern 4** – as we are used to a lot of disapproval from our parents, we create disapproval in our partners
>
> **Pattern 5** – you tend to get even with your parents through your partner
>
> **Pattern 6** – because of guilt or self-disapproval, we tend to 'beat ourselves up' using our relationships
>
> **Pattern 7** – you will always find someone who fits your patterns.

There are a few more, but I have listed the ones that

underline the self-reflecting nature of relationships. If you think about each of these patterns, as your partner reflects each of these back to you, think of the immense possibilities for self-discovery here!

I hope you haven't taken any of this to mean that we begin a relationship with the idea in mind of changing our partner. It is utterly impossible to change anyone but ourselves. But if you both go into a relationship with the realisation that changes are possible and desirable, then the space is created for you both to change and grow.

Naturally, the fear arises, 'What if we grow in different directions; what if we grow apart?'

It may happen. Life is full of risks, and this is one of them. Equally, it may not. Remember that a strong attraction to someone means that you have a lot of patterns in common, and it may take a long time (like a lifetime) to work through them all!

As a relationship exists to help us get through our patterns, the ultimate goal is to work through those which keep our relationships from being pleasurable and fulfilling at the same time as we are growing.

If your relationship does end, Sondra Ray reminds us that the next relationship is always going to be better than the last. This doesn't mean, by the way, that the next relationship will necessarily be as difficult as the last, but all of the growth you have experienced in your current relationship, will never have to be redone!

So, do we ever finish? No, not until the Universe fulfills its own patterns. Remember that we are an internal part of the Universe and its workings, and until the Universe is complete, neither can we be.

What happens then? Do we always have to suffer to grow? No, we don't. But until we get through the patterns related to our own dense bodies, it will be painful. As we move through these patterns and into the more subtle levels of growth, we find something new. Growth is no longer painful, and becomes less and less uncomfortable. Why, it is even *pleasurable*!

Remember Lowen's remark in chapter 5: 'The feeling of pleasure that stems from a natural and undisturbed rhythm of life embraces all our activities and relationships.'

As we dissolve our unharmonious patterns through our

relationships, a new harmony begins to emerge: the harmony that was inside us all along, the rhythm of the Cosmos, the beat of the Stars.

Our partners are truly our pathway back to the Stars.

Chapter 8

SOCIAL AND ECONOMIC CYCLES AND RHYTHMS

> Until human nature changes materially, there is not
> likely to be abandonment of the law of expansion and
> contraction in business.
>
> CHARLES H DOW

Man is, without a doubt, a highly social animal. Our
mutual survival as a species has, to a very high degree,
been dependent on our co-operative nature.

Exactly where we fit in the social scale of other animals
is a little hard to pin down, yet it is important that we try
in order to understand how our lives are part of the
greater scheme of things. It is our individual and personal
understanding of ourselves that is important, and how
our own, unique life, is part of a greater pattern. This
comes not from reading, but from self-understanding;
from inner, rather than outer experience.

We are programmed to a large degree by our biology,
whether we like it or not. We are not all that far removed
as a species from our savannah-dwelling hunter-ancestors.
Our cells are their cells, our instincts are their instincts.

Our ancestors survived by co-operative hunting (today
we call it 'working'), while the women tended the fires
(today it is called home-making). There are still woolly
mammoths to be slain (the next big contract), still pred-
ators lurking (the taxman). All that has changed are the
costumes.

Most of the way our societies are organised, from our
family structure to the structure of corporations, has a firm
grounding in our biology. Organic structures are the order
of the day.

Lewis Thomas takes a rather amused (but perhaps not
totally inaccurate) view of human social activities:

> Viewed from a suitable height, the aggregating clusters of
> medical scientists . . . have the look of social insects. There
> is the same vibrating, ionic movement . . . (touching)
> antennae and exchange of small bits of information . . . If
> the boards were not nailed down, it would not be a surprise to
> see them put together a nest of sorts.[1]

They do, in fact, remind one of a swarm of ants, although
it is not particularly acceptable to say so! But:

> Ants are so much like human beings as to be an embarrass-
> ment. They farm fungi, raise aphids as livestock, launch
> armies into wars, use chemical sprays to alarm and confuse
> enemies, capture slaves . . . They exchange information
> ceaselessly. They do everything but watch television.[2]

Although this is a bit tongue in cheek, it does serve to
underline how much human behaviour is interconnected
to the behaviour of other species.

Remember what I have emphasised in previous chapters:
that a great deal of what takes places in the rhythmic
nature of life is connected to the rhythms of individual
cells. Each cell in your body is effectively a separate organism. About 600 trillion of them have come together in a
social, co-operative organisation that is *your body*.

Cells remember, cells sense, cells communicate. Would
it be such a surprise to learn that our total organism takes
its basic patterns from the unique components which
make it up. Just like the Universe we live in.

In fact, the one (and virtually the *only* one) thing which
sets us apart genetically from other species is our language,
our ability to recognise and analyse patterns. Most other
human pattern-making activity stems from it: art, music,
architecture, government and business organisation,
science, medicine.

Thomas says:

> If language is at the core of our social existence, holding us
> together, housing us in meaning, it may also be safe to say
> that art and music are functions of the same Universal,
> genetically determined mechanism. If we are social crea-
> tures because of this, and therefore like ants, I for one do
> not mind.[3]

SOCIAL AND ECONOMIC CYCLES AND RHYTHMS

Nor do I. Although human culture is enormously varied, there are a great number of patterns and cycles that are common to all human life.

I was made profoundly aware of how much we all have in common some years ago whilst travelling in India. I was on a train from Bombay to Poona (where the carriages all have signs saying 'please do not light cooking fires in the carriage'!), and I was sitting talking to a lovely Indian gentleman.

The conversation finally came around to the state of things in the world generally. Suddenly I heard him saying: 'Aah, I just don't know what is happening to life in India. The politicians are all crooked, the children no longer respect their elders, and the rupee just won't buy what it used to!'

I had heard this conversation before! In America: in England: in Australia!

Suddenly, it really struck me – how alike we all are!

There is a great deal of communication that passes back and forth through body signals that are common to all cultures, and are rooted in pre-verbal infancy. Screams, whimpers, laughs, roars and moans convey the same messages vocally. Next time you have an opportunity to watch a foreign-language film on TV turn off the dubbed translation and see how much you can understand just from the body language. These are patterns that are clearly understood by anyone, and serve to underline the similarities we have with people of all cultures.

In every human culture the Universal patterns repeat themselves: expansion and contraction; movement into complexity; movement into density (try dealing with an entrenched bureaucracy!), and so on.

Within the social cycles of each society, the future never simply recycles the past. Each new cycle is another stage of growth onward from the last. History has an ebb and flow, an expansion and contraction pattern.

This has been strongly identified in American history by Arthur Schlesinger Jr., who has seen that in the past 100 years, American history has undergone the same basic cycle several times – a period of economic depression, war, social change and activism, usually followed by a period of backlash, consolidation, relative calm and prosperity.

These cycles recur uncannily every thirty years. Schlesinger believes that these cycles are based on generations in that people have usually absorbed their formative political views by the time that they are 18 or so.

The overall pattern is one from private interest to public purpose; from self-interest to public interest.[4] Expansion and contraction.

The Babylonians under Hammurabi went from a city to an empire in one generation, and then back to a city again in another generation or two.

The Assyrians, under Sennacherib and Assurbanipal, rose from the city-state of Nineveh to envelop the Nile, and then collapsed back to Nineveh after a generation. Finally even Nineveh fell.

The Greeks under Phillip II and Alexander, expanded from the humble backwater of Macedonia, eventually to reach India; only to break up again into three bickering provinces within a few years after Alexander's death.

So too with the Roman, and later the British, Empires, which took many generations and tons of treasure to build, only to collapse inwards on themselves in less than a generation.

These are but a few examples; others can be found on all continents, at all periods of history, and in all cultures.

Were they acts of futility? To expand only to collapse again? Perhaps not. Let us look to the nature of things for an answer.

An oak tree sheds thousands of acorns to produce just one new tree; a dandelion spreads hundreds of seeds on the wind to produce one new plant; billions of human sperm are produced to create only one new human body. An inner burst of energy to expand and scatter the seeds of something new.

I am certain that the pattern of human history has followed the same process – new ideas, new cultures, new bloodlines, all being spread through migration and conquest. War and conquest seem to be a radical and painful way to accomplish this, but what were the historic alternatives?

For the most part until recently, resources have been scarce, particularly food. To welcome any number of newcomers would have meant starvation; thus the resistance to migration and change.

However, in the last century, we have seen the beginning of a true 'cultural revolution'. With the advent of efficient sailing ships, then steam power, then the aeroplane, the movement of peoples in large numbers from one place to another became a practical reality; this is combined with the agricultural revolution so that food resources were no longer a problem. At least in the Northern Hemisphere the barriers are disappearing to the mixing of peoples without the need for bloodshed.

It is a beginning.

We are also at a time of beginning in our understanding of the interconnection of all peoples. The famines in several African countries at the time of a vast EEC food surplus served to underline the absurd way in which we live with one another. How ironic, with all of the self-important ministers, administrators, officials and diplomats, our awareness of this had to be underlined by a scruffy rock star! In times of real crisis, real human beings, no matter what their outer appearance, always come forth.

Surplus and famine are, of course, part of the ebb and flow, the expansion and contraction. It is the nature of things that these will occur, although this doesn't mean that we must be victim to them. Quite the contrary – it is a chance to open our hearts to giving in a time of plenty, and open our hearts to receiving in a time of want: *both* increase our Humanity.

Economies within various cultures also undergo an expansion and contraction cycle. As soon as this is understood, many of the social problems such as unemployment may disappear. When the economy is in a contraction stage, everyone must contract financially. If wages are maintained at the old level by some (or as is often the case, even *higher* wages are demanded) the contraction will simply squeeze out those for whom there is no money left.

This new approach to economics will, of course, require a massive re-adjustment of thinking at all levels of society. There is no point in contracting wages if mortgages or time-payments stay the same, or if interest rates remain high.

Ultimately, however, if these cycles are not recognised and acknowledged, the same pattern will continue; when there is too much squeeze on an economy it shatters – this results in a depression.

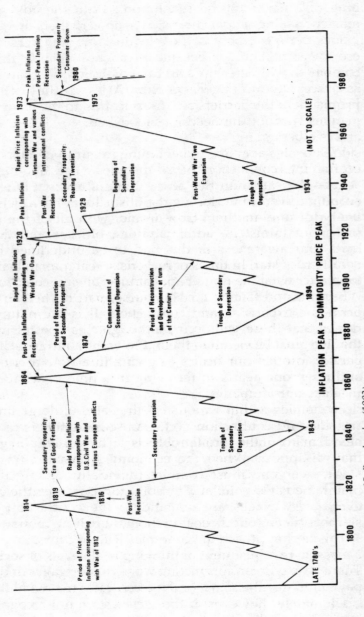

FOUR LONG WAVE CYCLES 1780 - 2000

Period of Price Inflation corresponding with War of 1812

Secondary Prosperity "Era of Good Feelings"

Rapid Price Inflation corresponding with U.S Civil War and various European conflicts

Post-War Recession

Post-Peak Inflation Recession

Period of Reconstruction and Secondary Prosperity

Rapid Price Inflation corresponding with World War One

Peak Inflation

Post-War Recession

Secondary Prosperity: "Roaring Twenties"

Rapid Price Inflation corresponding with Vietnam War and various international conflicts

Peak Inflation 1973

Post-Peak Inflation Recession

Secondary Prosperity Consumer Boom

Commencement of Secondary Depression

Beginning of Secondary Depression

Period of Reconstruction and Development at turn of the Century

Secondary Depression

Trough of Secondary Depression

Trough of Secondary Depression

Post-World War Two Expansion

Trough of Depression

1814 1819 1816 1864 1874 1894 1920 1929 1934 1973 1975 1980

LATE 1780's 1800 1820 1840 1843 1860 1880 1900 1920 1940 1960 1980

INFLATION PEAK = COMMODITY PRICE PEAK

(NOT TO SCALE)

From R. Beckman, Downwave, p. 15, Pan, London (1983).

SOCIAL AND ECONOMIC CYCLES AND RHYTHMS

The history of the past 200 years clearly shows this cycle: a peak in the western economies, followed by a massive crash. A cycle that repeats about every fifty years.

This cycle was first noticed in the 1920's by a Russian economist, N D Kondratatieff, who was promptly sent to Siberia by a 'grateful' Russian government, who saw him as a threat to the regime. He didn't live to see his greatest prophecy fulfilled: the Great Depression of the 1930s.[5]

In his book *Downwave,* economist Robert Beckman looks at these cycles, in an attempt to forecast the next depression. On the previous page he presents a graph of the economic cycles since the late 1870s.

You will see from the chart that the cyclic nature of economic life is obvious. Economic fluctuations, however, are hardly a new thing; they have been epidemic in most societies throughout history. Even the Romans had problems with rampant inflation.

There is considerable evidence that many cycles of history are related to the weather cycles discovered by Dr Wheeler (chapter 2). Colder weather and longer dry periods will mean scarcer food (and higher prices) for the rich nations, starvation for the poorer ones. According to the 100 year cycle, the latter 1980's should be such a period. The African famines may well be the outworking of this cycle.

The figure on page 82 reproduces Dr Wheeler's 'drought clock', showing the weather cycles since ancient times, and clearly showing how times of social unrest and upheaval are connected to these cycles. These weather cycles may well be responsible for Kondratatieff's economic cycles.

We are, you will notice, already entering one of these cycles. How we will handle this is, of course, entirely up to us.

Other human institutions also tend to follow the pattern set by nature.

Organisations tend to evolve in an organic form, and follow patterns of development that are parallel to the evolution of our own species. Often at first, starting with a single person, like the first single cell organism to evolve in the primitive oceans. This cell performs all of its own functions – thinking, feeding, protecting, organising and so forth.

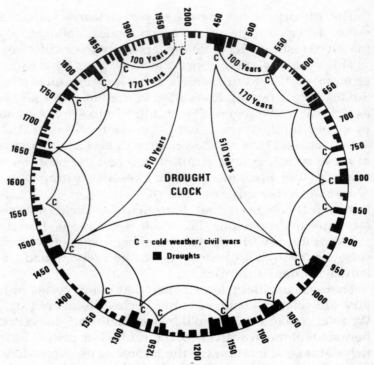

Dr Raymond Wheeler's Drought Clock

From R. Beckman, Downwave, *p. 123. Pan, London (1983).*

Then other cells (people) are attracted to perform specific functions. In the diagram, we will assume that the man is beginning a one-man company making a product. The parallels with other types of businesses will be obvious, I'm certain.

In Stage 1, the man and the single cell perform all of the functions, as mentioned.

In Stage 2, new cells (Men B to F) have been attracted and joined to perform specialised functions. Man A now spends most of his time directing other men, as Cell A does directing other cells. Cell A and Man A have become a primitive brain.

In Stage 3, the original cells (men) have become specialised controllers. In the company organism, Men A–F have become director and department heads (note the organic term here!), and Cells A–F have now become specialised brain cells.

SOCIAL AND ECONOMIC CYCLES AND RHYTHMS

The size of social organisms also seems to have 'organic' limits. If you have ever worked in a large expanding company, you will know that departments eventually become unwieldy as new people are added, and must finally divide to function efficiently.

This is not just true of companies – all human structures have natural, organic limits. Our evolution did not create or prepare us to live as a great mass of thousands of individuals. We are tribal in nature – designed to function in small units; probably a hundred or less. It is in our biology; locked in our genes.

The stresses of city-living are well-enough documented, but does this mean we shouldn't live in cities, or work in large groups?

Not at all. We have created a highly adaptive behaviour for mass living. It is our inner nature as primates to establish a dominance hierarchy; a pecking order. When we meet a mass of strangers on a daily basis, this is impossible, and our biology responds with stress. In adaptive behaviour we avoid the signals by which dominance is established – we avoid staring at one another, pointing or gesturing in another's direction, avoiding physical contact. Only in this way can we manage to survive in an otherwise over-stimulating social environment.[6]

In a company, business, or organisational situation, the hierarchy usually grows organically – Cell B/Person B moves up to manager or foreman, and so on. But as sections or departments begin to grow in numbers, the restlessness begins to set in, who is above me, who is below?

You may have been in offices or work situations where there are only two or three others – and haven't you just been aware of who comes first!

In terms of our own human evolution, Lilian Verner-Bonds has pointed out that this is a time when men have an opportunity to move from being a tribal 'herd animal', to a true biological evolution into our own uniqueness – which also creates the space for everyone else to do the same.

Thus it is internal pressure of the most basic sort that creates organisations, government, businesses, and living organisms. The same forces that on a larger scale drive the Cosmos.

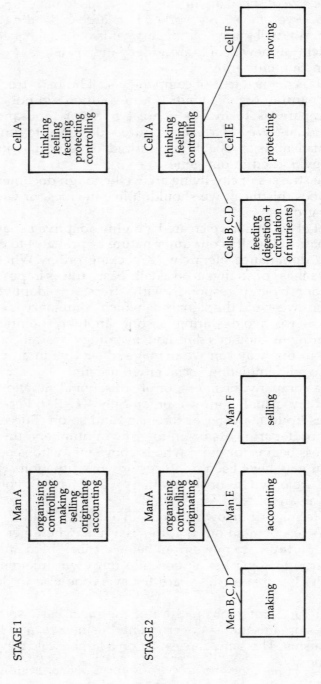

STAGE 3

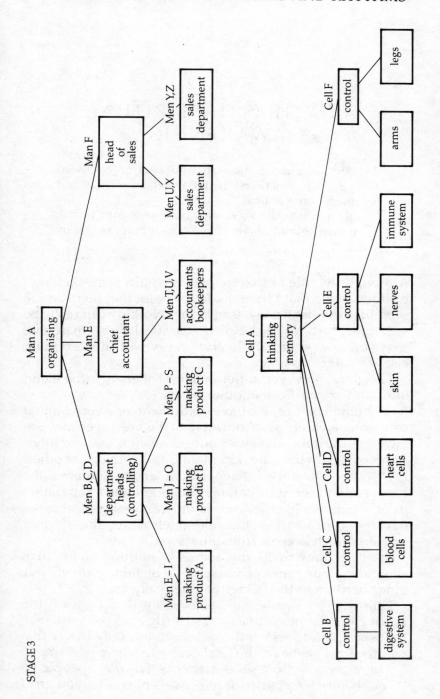

Chapter 9

RHYTHMS OF SPIRITUAL AWAKENING

I died to the inorganic state and became endowed with growth, and then I died to vegetable growth and attained to the animal.

I died from Animality and became Adam (man): why then should I fear? When have I become less by dying?

RUMI (*Mathnawi, Book III*)

Although the title of this chapter is 'spiritual awakening', by now I hope that I have made the point that there are no separate and distinct levels of being. Nothing can really be separated out to be labelled specifically as 'material', 'physical', or 'spiritual'. Everything is part of everything else – *nothing is separate*.

There are, however, different levels of energy that blend into, and are part of, all other levels.

As human beings, we have on the whole, a very limited conscious awareness of ourselves. We are especially unaware of the subtle levels of our own being that are interconnected with the other kingdoms, and with one another.

In other chapters I have talked about some of the barriers that keep us separate. This is not just a separation from others – which in itself is only an externalisation of our inner processes – but ultimately it is these inner barriers which keep us from ourselves.

Spiritual growth in my view, is nothing more than expanding our view of ourselves – of taking down our inner barriers to the Being that we really are.

Ultimately, our external beliefs about the godhead, the prophets, churches, rituals and so forth, are irrelevant. I say irrelevant, not to lessen those beliefs, but only to say that whatever you believe, the final goal is to *believe in yourself*.

There are a distinct set of patterns that most people go through on the path to inner awakening. As you read through them, you will see that they are just a reflection of the same patterns I have talked about throughout the book. This is because all things are part of everything else, *my growth is a result of someone else's, and someone else's is a result of mine.*

Someone else has taken the first steps and evolved the processes and techniques that have helped me to remove my own inner barriers. In doing so I have had new insights that will help others.

We can take this to an even larger scale, and realise that, because each of us is an integral part of the Universe, my growth is part of the growth of the entire Universe. Because the Universe is a growing Being, as the Universe grows, so must I.

Is it any wonder the pressures for growth are so irresistible? Because the inner urge for awakening is so strong, we are easily propelled into that which promises 'instant enlightenment' – drugs, gurus, cults, and so on. Once again, we step into 'who we are not', but this time at a different level.

At the **Beginning** stage of the awakening process, we often slip into the old pattern of an external authority source: our parents, because we usually haven't come to recognise ourselves as our own ultimate source in other areas of our lives.

We slip into paternalistic (or maternalistic) religions, or cults with a strong authority figure, or gurus. In every case, the authority for our own lives still comes from outside: the 'thou shalt nots'; if you follow the rules, God (or the guru, or whoever) will love you and take care of you, if not . . .

The impulse for change in our spiritual lives at the Beginning stage frequently comes from the view that something is wrong in our ordinary, everyday life, as if our everyday life were somehow separate from our spiritual life. There is often a feeling of, 'is this all there is?'

In my case, this meant a three-bedroom house, a red sports car, my own business, and a reasonably good income. I had the 'American Dream' – and I couldn't work out why I was so miserable. What was missing from the picture was *me*. So, like all pilgrims on the spiritual path, I set out on the quest to discover – me.

This is stage two in the pattern – the **Quest**.

As we are still used to thinking in externals at this early stage, the quest frequently begins as an outer quest, rather than an inner one. We are often not clear what it is that we are seeking, but our inner urge tells us to go *somewhere*. India, Europe, anywhere but where we are. We are seeking ourselves, and sooner or later we realise that although going to a new place 'outside' can teach us many things, as we are pulled away from those familiar safety nets that we have carefully woven for ourselves – nevertheless, the place we really needed to go, lies inside ourselves.

At each stage, there is the opportunity to get stuck; the quest is a beginning for some and an end for others. Many become perpetual seekers, never stopping their seeking long enough to do any finding.

In the next stage, that of **Discovery**, we come across the doorways to new inner worlds. At first the glimmers of the other side are so enticing and brilliant, that we believe that at last we have found *it*.

The early Discovery phase is a popular place to get stuck, especially if you have discovered levels of self-awareness which are often labelled as 'psychic'. Our limited experience here leads us to believe that we have some special gifts that others don't have. If our egos get involved in the act (which they usually do), we can remain stuck here for a long time.

This is the time when so many illusions are created. The ego gives us what we want to hear. We get fragments of truth that the ego then runs wild with, constructing all manner of elaborations on the tiniest fragments. As the ego gives itself what it wants, the illusions look so enticing that staying stuck here can be a lifetime occupation. Fortunately for most of us, reality eventually intrudes.

Fairly early in the Discovery stage, we begin to catch glimmers of Universal Truth. One of the first truths we discover is that *we are special*. However, at this stage, we usually miss the other half of that truth – *so is everyone else*.

We get very stuck on 'specialness' for good reason – 'specialness' has good survival value. It is part of our biological programming – the herd bull, the dominant male, the warrior chief – the 'special' ones get to mate. It is part of the nature of things, and we humans are hardly immune to the animal side of our nature – we are an intimate part of its cycles and rhythms.

So what's wrong with being special? Nothing really, as long as we are able to recognise and acknowledge everyone else's 'specialness', as long as we don't create separation, which is *not* the natural order.

Expansion and contraction cycles are prominent during the whole of the awakening process. Periods of deep introspection, followed by an almost explosive need to share our discoveries – a perfectly natural urge.

However, a popular place to get stuck in the Discovery stage is to become a teacher. People who get stuck on their own 'specialness' often stop here – I did. This is because yet another truth finally dawns: 'it is not possible for me to know what I know, and not share it with others'.

Now, there is nothing whatsoever wrong with this – it is an absolutely natural impulse – *as long as we don't stop learning ourselves*. But the teacher trap is in falling into the idea that you have the answers; and that you always have the right answers.

This, in a limited way, may be absolutely true – you may have the right answers – for *you*; and possibly for those who are attracted to your teaching. But in this phase, we don't yet realise that *there are lots of right answers*.

Another aspect of the teacher trap phase is the discovery that you are the Christ (or the Buddha or whatever). Of course you are. *But so is everyone else.*

Christhood is a state of pure self-acceptance, and every human being has the potential to realise it fully. One aspect of Christhood is that the inner door to the Source is open – ultimately it is the same Source for us all.

This is a tempting place to stop – to notice your own Christhood, but not anyone else's. I got stuck on this one for a while too. Lots of people do. Most gurus still are. When a guru tells you 'I am God', he doesn't usually mean '. . . and so are you'.

Another common belief that appears during the Discovery stage is that you were a fallen angel. Many even believe that they were Satan or Lucifer. Once again, a grain of truth.

If we see Lucifer as an archetype, a Great Being fallen from Grace, then every single person on the Earth is

Lucifer. We are *all* Great Beings and, at a deep level, we all believe ourselves fallen from Grace, from connection to our Source.

Earlier I mentioned what I believe to be a common experience of all men – the feeling of abandonment by God for taking on a body; a feeling of being cast out of a place of total safety, where all of our basic needs are met all of the time; the Garden of Eden. We re-create this experience in our birth; we are cast out of the all-supplying womb, to realise that we are separate from the source of our supply.

I believe this experience to be the root of the Shadow Self, our own dark side, the side that we literally are afraid to expose to the light. *All* of us have a shameful secret – we all believe ourselves to be fallen angels.

The underlying pattern of each and every one of our lives is to resolve the separate feeling – we are, everyone of us, ultimately and finally alone. Paradoxically, in our utter aloneness, we discover our Self; the Self that is ultimately everyone's Self; the Self that is the Universe and all things in it. Out of our aloneness comes Unity. As I said earlier on, we often know a thing best by experiencing its opposite.

What, finally, are we developing *towards*? I have used the term Christhood here, but the term is really a metaphor for whatever your own highest aspiration is. There are many names for it; Christhood is only one of them.

I believe my own ultimate goal is to become *Human*. The world is full of people, but not so many humans. My friend and publisher Michael Mann recently told me of a dream he had, which sums up my own purpose quite well.

He was drawn, somewhat bewildered, through a tall and slightly menacing wood to a clearing. In that clearing was a ring of all the animals on the Earth, from the tiny vole to the larger deer and elk. All of them were speaking to him, and in particular he remembered the rabbit, who, in being on the Earth, had fully developed its own 'rabbitness'. And so it was for all the other animals. The vole had developed fully its own 'voleness', the deer its own 'deerness'. Of all the animals in the circle, only one had utterly failed to develop.

'Humanness' is what is lacking in this world. In my own spiritual quest, I sought to find the part of myself that was God. When I found it, I found that I had had it all along, as do all men. There are many parts to our own godliness – creativity, compassion, love. We all have these things, but in many of us they are masked, because we have failed to develop our 'Humanness'.

I discovered that being God was easy – being Human is difficult.

I believe that to become Human is the final stage of every man's quest. It is not something already inside us, like our godliness, but rather something we are here to develop.

Man is capable of an amazingly complex series of relationships, as we have touched on in the preceding chapters. We have also seen that those relationships follow patterns, and that ultimately they follow the patterns of the Universe itself.

Man is a reflection of the Universe, through its patterns.

I have also said that pattern recognition is a key to being Human; but why should man have this ability in particular?

We know we are a species trying to move beyond our own biologically programmed limitations in order to grow, and really at a more basic level, even just to survive. As human population increases, so do the tensions generated by our own biology. Human institutions are increasingly stretched to accommodate a biology not at all created for the lives we live today.

We know likewise that evolution is a universal pattern and that like all creatures on the Earth, we too must evolve. Desmond Morris reminds us that many exciting species have come and gone on the Earth; and so too, must we. It is the nature of things.

With genetic engineering in the human species a real possibility, perhaps one goal of life in giving us the ability to recognise patterns, is *to be able to control our own evolution.*

Many of you will find this idea terrifying. And so you should. We know enough about our own patterns already to recognise the astronomical potential for disaster.

However man is, by his nature, a risk-taking creature. I

think this is one risk we will eventually take. Perhaps this is even one thing that we have been created *for*.

The Universe itself is evolving: it needs to evolve. Perhaps we are moving into a position to be a more conscious part of that pattern of evolution. Like it or not, we are now an integral part of the evolution of almost all life on Earth. There are few places on the Earth that we as a species do not dominate. We do this mostly unconsciously, although the ecology movement in recent years has begun to recognise how interconnected all life on Earth really is. The fate of a particular tree in the Amazon rain forest is as much a part of your life as what you had for breakfast; less immediate, but no less important.

'I am not my brother's keeper' is a lie. We are all one another's keepers, because our brothers are us. 'Do unto others as you would have done unto you', takes on a whole new meaning. *As you do to others, so you do unto yourself.*

Why should all of this take place in stages – cycles of growth. Fundamentally, this is because growth is painful. Gail Sheehy says of human growth:

> We are not unlike a particularly hardy crustacean. The lobster grows by developing and shedding a series of hard, protective shells. Each time it expands from within, the confining shell must be sloughed off. It is left exposed and vulnerable until, in time, a new covering grows to replace the old.[1]

Growth always involves moving through barriers – physical, mental and spiritual. This requires energy; energy creates tension; tension and its release are painful. This is why growth moves in rhythms and cycles – cycles create the tension for growth.

Imagine the energy that goes into the growth of your physical body over a period of 17 or 18 years. Then imagine that happening all at once. From a single cell to a full adult, in an instant. Should we expect the growth of the spiritual side of our nature to be any different?

It is not part of the nature of things to have instant *anything*.

Remember, the Universe is *still* creating itself after fifteen thousand million years.

Perhaps this need to grow in stages is the underlying pattern of reincarnation, (if indeed reincarnation exists). I have been a past-life therapist myself; I have seen hundreds of past-life memories that have arisen spontaneously in various courses. There is, without question, a body of memories from the past that are accessible to us. But are they *ours*?

I still don't know the final answer to this. Life is an energy flow, so it must be continuous. Our lives have existed in one form or another as long as the Universe has existed. Our lives on the Earth are a bit like the crest of a wave – all the froth at the surface, but with very deep water indeed underlying it all. The froth is any one incarnation – and when the froth is gone, it moves on to become a new wave, new froth, but underlying it is the same great body of water, the same great body of energy from which all things are created.

As each of our lives has its own unique pattern, there will be a natural resonance between that pattern and patterns like it. It may well be that through that resonance, we have access to *any* memory that has a like pattern. There is no reason, of course, why those past patterns couldn't be ours.

Our own life on the Earth is part of another cycle, connected to raising the consciousness of the planet itself. The cycle looks like this:

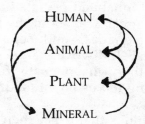

Mineral matter is elevated in consciousness through its incorporation in the plant kingdom. Plant matter is further elevated in consciousness through its incorporation in the animal and human kingdoms. All these kingdoms eventually return their mineral matter to the Earth.

The kingdoms, then are a mechanism for the cyclic

incorporation of the matter of the Earth into higher and higher states of consciousness.

As we have discovered, the Universe is moving into more complex patterns and relationships. As it does so, it develops its own needs for growth – beyond just its physical body – as we do.

I have used the word God (the Universe) a lot, without really defining the word. Perhaps it seems a strange need, to define God. But I believe and feel that God is a Being who is, as we are, seeking a definition of Himself.

Remember, the Universe is a place that has just begun – the movement into density is in its very early stages yet. The Universe could potentially develop for at least 10,000 times its current age. Whatever God may be, the Universe is part of His creation, and there is still a lot of creating yet to be done. If God and Man are one through our mutual patterns, then God must have a need for growth also – and the final goal of growth is Self-discovery.

I believe that the Universe is the physical body of God. That God is a collective Being, made of all that exists in the Universe, both manifest and unmanifest.

If God is a learning being, then what better way to learn about creating, than to have parts of yourself that also create, but create independently from each other, so each is its own experience of creation. If, perhaps, the Earth is populated by four billion creators, then each day, God can experience four billion new ways to create. Multiply that by the number of inhabited planets in the Universe . . .

I have talked a great deal about the need to resolve our own feelings of 'aloneness' and 'separateness'. If we are part of God's own Self-discovery and learning through our mutual patterns, then what does this fundamental need of every human being tell us about God?

God is also alone.

If you are all things that exist, then what else is there? Nothing. You are totally alone.

Perhaps this is the most basic Universal pattern of all. If you think of it, God has also taken on a body, and in doing so has created a sense of 'separateness'. Stars are separate from planets which are separate from men.

How does the Universe resolve its own 'separateness'? Perhaps it seeks the answer through us.

NOTES

Chapter 1

1. Bertsch, George, 'Vibrations of the Atom', *Scientific American*, v. 248, no. 5, p. 41, May 1983

Chapter 2

1. Bernard, P, 'Le cycle solaire dans l'agitation microséismique', *C.R.A.S.*, CCVI, p. 1585 1938
2. Brierley, D and Davies, J, 'Lunar Influence on Meteor Rates', *Journal of Geophysical Research*, LXVIII, no. 5, p. 1401 1963

Chapter 3

1. Gauquelin, Michel, *The Cosmic Clocks*, p. 126
2. ibid., p. 133
3. ibid., p. 136
4. Whitman, John, *The Psychic Power of Plants*, p. 134
5. Beckman, Robert, *Downwave*, pp. 6, 7
6. Blair, Elizabeth, 'Changing Wavelengths', *You*, p. 127, Oct. 18, 1987
7. Brown, F A, Jr, *Biological Clocks*
8. Semenko, A D, 'Short term memory in plants', *Doklady Akademii Naut SSSR*, Vol. 183, No. 2, pp. 476–478, Nov. 1968
9. Rettallack, Dorothy, *The Sound of Music and Plants*, p. 60
10. Thomas, Lewis, *The Lives of a Cell*, p. 23
11. Thomas, ibid., p. 24
12. Morris, Desmond, *The Naked Ape*, p. 119
13. ibid., 26
14. Morowitz, H J, *Energy Flow in Biology: Biological Organization as a Problem in Thermal Physics*
15. Whitman, John, *The Psychic Power of Plants*, p. 22
16. Thompkins, Peter and Bird, C, *The Secret Life of Plants*, p. 22
17. Whitman, John, ibid., p. 32
18. ibid., p. 34
19. ibid., p. 77
20. ibid., p. 79
21. Backster, Cleve, 'Evidence of Primary Reception in Plant Life', *International Journal of Parapsychology*, Vol. X, no. 4, 330, 1968

Chapter 4

1. Thomas, Lewis, *The Lives of a Cell*, p. 1
2. Gauquelin, Michel, *The Cosmic Clocks*, p. 155
3. ibid., p. 158
4. ibid., p. 158
5. ibid., p. 160
6. Blair, Elizabeth, 'Changing Wavelengths', *You*, pp. 126, 127, Oct. 18, 1987
7. Graham, Kate, *Moon Madness*, Company Magazine
8. Gauquelin, ibid., p. 164
9. ibid., p. 164
10. ibid., pp. 165, 166
11. Lowen, Alexander, *Pleasure*, p. 238
12. ibid.
13. ibid., p. 72
14. Panati, Charles, *Breakthrough*, Pan and Macmillan
15. Morris, Desmond, *The Naked Ape*, p. 121

Chapter 5

1. Lowen, Alexander, *Pleasure*, p. 236
2. Gauquelin, Michel, *Astrology and Science*, p. 163
3. ibid., p. 166
4. ibid., p. 167
5. ibid., p. 168
6. Gauquelin, *The Cosmic Clocks*, p. 88
7. ibid., pp. 88–91

Chapter 6

1. Verny, Thomas, *The Secret Life of the Unborn Child*, p. 63
2. ibid., p. 63
3. ibid., p. 101
4. Sheehy, Gail, *Passages*, p. 39, Bantam Books, London, 1976
5. ibid., p. 166
6. ibid., p. 351
7. ibid., p. 361
8. ibid., p. 364

Chapter 7

1. Sheehy, Gail, *Passages*, p. 129, Bantam Books, London, 1976

Chapter 8

1. Thomas, Lewis, *The Lives of a Cell*, p. 11
2. ibid., p. 12

NOTES

3. ibid., p. 106
4. Morrow, Lance, *Time*, Mar 30, 1987
5. Beckman, Robert, *Downwave*, p. 13
6. Morris, Desmond, *The Naked Ape*, p. 162

Chapter 9

1. Sheehy, Gail, *Passages*, p. 29, Bantam Books, London, 1976

BIBLIOGRAPHY

Beckman, Robert, *Downwave* (Pan Books, London, 1983)

Brown, F A, Jr, *Biological Clocks* (American Institute of Biological Sciences, Boston, 1962)

Gauquelin, Michel, *Astrology and Science* (Peter Davies, London, 1969)

Gauquelin, Michel, *The Cosmic Clocks* (Peter Owen, London, 1967)

Humble, Richard, *Warfare in the Ancient World* (London Book Club Associates, 1980)

Morowitz, H J, *Energy Flow in Biology: Biological Organization as a Problem in Thermal Physics* (Academic Press, New York, 1968)

Morris, Desmond, *The Naked Ape* (Corgi, London, 1967)

Ornstein, Robert, *Multimind* (Macmillan, London, 1986)

Panati, Charles, *Breakthrough* (Pan Books Ltd)

Ray, Sondra, *Loving Relationships* (Celestial Arts, Berkely, 1980)

Retallack, Dorothy, *The Sound of Music and Plants*, (DeVorss & Co., Santa Monica, 1973)

Thomas, Lewis, *The Lives of a Cell* (Bantam, New York, 1974)

Thompkins, Peter and Bird, Christopher, *The Secret Life of Plants* (Harper and Row, New York, 1973)

Verny, Dr Thomas, 1982, *The Secret Life of the Unborn Child*, (Sphere, London, 1982)

Whitman, John, *The Psychic Power of Plants* (Star Books, London 1974)